CraftArtist User Guide

How to Contact Us

Our main office
(UK, Europe):

The Software Centre
PO Box 2000, Nottingham,
NG11 7GW, UK

Main: (0115) 914 2000

Registration (UK only): (0800) 376 1989

Sales (UK only): (0800) 376 7070

Customer Service/
Technical Support: http://www.support.serif.com/

General Fax: (0115) 914 2020

North American office
(USA, Canada):

The Software Center
17 Hampshire Drive,
Suites 1 & 2,
Hudson NH 03051, USA

Main: (603) 889-8650

Registration: (800) 794-6876

Sales: (800) 489-6703

Customer Service/
Technical Support: http://www.support.serif.com/

General Fax: (603) 889-1127

Online

Visit us on the Web at: http://www.serif.com/

International

Please contact your local distributor/dealer. For further details, please contact us
at one of our phone numbers above.

Contents

Welcome

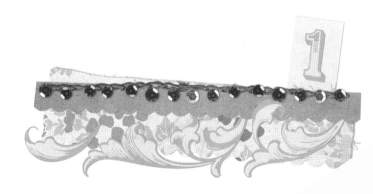

Welcome to Craft Artist

Welcome to CraftArtist—the digital crafting solution that combines crafting fun with a wealth of powerful drawing and crafting tools for the very best results. In an instant, you'll be able to create beautiful print projects with that professional touch!

Projects such as **greeting cards**, **scrapbooks**, **photobooks**, **stationery**, **gift wrap**, and **party crafts** can be created from ready-to-go layouts or from scratch—it's your choice!

For unlimited design possibilities, CraftArtist works with a range of **DaisyTrail Digikits**, each offering themed items that you can use as starting points for your projects. Each Digikit includes a selection of drag-and-drop **layouts**, **backgrounds**, **embellishments**, **materials**, **photo frames**, and decorative **letters**.

In addition to supplying ready-to-go content, CraftArtist lets you add decorative **lines**, **shapes**, and **stencils**. You can also apply natural or spray **brush strokes** using easy-to-use drawing and painting tools. Photos can be added to your project, and image adjustments and effects applied using the powerful **PhotoLab**. You can even cut out the subject of a photo, and create your own photo frames!

Once you've created your masterpiece, you'll want to share it. A lively web-based craft designing community—**www.daisytrail.com**—is available for you to share your projects freely or to selected groups. You'll make some new friends along the way too!

Don't forget to visit DaisyTrail.com to download your free Digikits—and purchase new ones!

Key features

Crafting essentials

- **Create beautiful craft projects easily!** (p. 18)
  Create **greetings cards, photobooks, stationery**, and **gift wrap** from your purchased Digikits. Simply select, edit, then print! Why not try **Make & Do projects** with step-by-step written and video instructions—create real greeting cards for friends and family!

- **Digikits** (p. 51)
  Digikits are rich in items perfect for craft designs. Your items, chosen from a powerful **Digikit Browser**, are loaded into **Content tabs** ready to drag and drop onto the page—nothing could be easier! You can increase the number of Digikits available to you by browsing and purchasing the latest Digikits hosted on the **www.daisytrail.com** website.

- **Scissor cuts, erasing, and adding to items** (p. 179)
  Take your 'virtual' scissors to materials with the **Scissors tool**—choose from a wide selection of scissor cut types (Square, Pinking, Shark Fin, ZigZag, and more). Use the **Erase** and **Freeform Paint** tools to remove and add to items.

- **Add impact with a ready-to-go stencil** (p. 201)
  The **Stencils** tab provides a wide selection of ready-to-go stencil templates—designs include birds, people, plants, shapes, and more. The stencils are quick and easy to use, and provide endless opportunities for creativity. Simply drag and drop your chosen stencil onto your page, then paint over it with the **Brush tool**, or use it to cut out a design from a photograph.

- **Design, print, and upload in high-resolution**
  In CraftArtist, 300dpi native working is the norm. All craft items are high-resolution so quality is guaranteed. Printing and upload at 300dpi gives truly outstanding high-quality output.

- **Layer work made easy**
  For greater design control, store items on **layers**—work on items on one layer without affecting items on other layers. Layers can be created, merged, and hidden, and display a hierarchical tree view of associated items for easy selection. Apply paper textures to layer items (p. 148)!

Ease of use

- **Total ease of use**
  Tabbed, collapsible, and dockable **Studio tabs** are always at hand. Choose from preset colors, line styles, brushes, and effects, or create your own. Use tabs to arrange, transform, and align items.

- **Context toolbars**
  Context toolbars offer different tools and options depending on the currently selected item. Great for efficiency and simplifying your workflow.

- **Design aids** (p. 70)
  Rotate your canvas through any angle, just like an artist would do in real life. For more focused design, use **Solo Mode** to work on items in isolation. Use the **Rule of Thirds** tool on your photos or on your project's pages for improved page composition.

Photos

- **Adding photos** (p. 77)
  Personalize your projects by **importing your own photos** from hard disk, CD/DVD, digital camera or scanner. Store photos in the **Photos tab** before dragging directly onto a page or into a photo frame; optionally fill each photo frame automatically using **AutoFlow**! At any time, try dragging a frame onto an unframed photo or swap one frame for another by drag-and-drop.

- **Cropping and fitting photos to frames** (p. 108)
  Use the **Crop Tool** to remove unwanted areas of your framed photo. For perfect photo placement, you can **scale**, **pan**, and **rotate** photos to your liking.

- **Frame Editor** allows you to create your own Digikit photo frames from a photo-based image of a frame.

- **Convert photos to frameless frames** (p. 116)
  Photos you've added directly to your page (i.e., those that are not inside a decorative photo frame) can be converted so that they sit inside "frameless" frames. These frames function exactly like the decorative frames you've added from the **Frames** tab, allowing you to crop, zoom, and pan the photos inside them. You can even use the **AutoFlow** feature to automatically replace frame contents!

- **Apply photo adjustments and effects** (p. 88)
  PhotoLab provides an impressive selection of editable non-destructive photo adjustments (**White Balance**, **Lighting**, **Curves**, to name just a few...) and creative effects (including a selection of artistic effects such as **Pencil**, **Watercolor**, and **Oil**).

  You can apply single or multiple filters to an entire photo, or to selected areas using a mask. Your original photo remains intact. You can even save adjustment/effect combinations as **Favorites** for future use.

PhotoLab also includes **Red-eye** and **Spot-repair** tools for easy retouching. (See *Applying PhotoLab filters* on p. 89.)

- **Photo cutouts** (p. 97)
  Cutout Studio makes light work of cutting out your photos. Use brushes to discard backgrounds (sky, walls, etc.) or keep subjects of interest (people, objects, etc.).

- Use **QuickFrame**, an ornate QuickShape, to frame your photos.

Brushes and Lines

- **Realistic brush strokes** (p. 205)
  Unleash the painter within you with CraftArtist's powerful **Brush tool**! Apply **natural** or **spray** brush strokes using preset brush types from the Brush tab's galleries—additionally pick brushes from Digikits. Even apply a brush stroke around item edges!

- **Natural brush strokes** (p. 208)
  The **Natural Media** category hosts **Acrylic**, **Charcoal**, **Paint**, **Felt Tip**, and **Watercolor** brushes. Use **Embroidery** brushes on cut materials, or why not adorn your page with lace and ribbon **Photo** brush effects which can be recolored in an instant.

- **Spray brush strokes** (p. 208)
  Have fun with **spray brushes** from categories such as **Airbrush**, **Embroidery**, **Flowers**, **Fun & Celebrations**, **Glitter**, and more.

- **Versatile line and curve drawing** (p. 160)
  For natural smooth curves, click and drag with the **Pen tool**, even edit Bezier curve segments with selectable join options. Draw straight or freeform lines with the **Pencil tool**. Join any line's ends to create irregular filled shapes, with optional offset outlines!

- **Brushes and lines get pressure sensitive!**
  Use in-built pressure sensitivity control for beautiful and realistic natural brush strokes or when drawing **freeform lines**; control the **weight** and **opacity** of your strokes as you apply pressure.

Text

- **Sentiments for that special message** (p. 137)
  Struggling to find the right words for your card? CraftArtist comes with **pre-written** and **pre-formatted sentiments** you can add to your cards with ease. Select **birthday greetings**, **quotes**, and messages for every occasion. If you've typed your own special message, save it as a **custom** sentiment for future use.

- **Artistic and shape text** (p. 119)
  Apply artistic text or text within QuickShapes right on the page... apply basic formatting from the always-at-hand Text context toolbar. Convert text to curves for text design freedom.

- **Fitting text to a path** (p. 130)
  Make your text flow along **drawn curves**, or even around **closed shapes** or **QuickShapes. Preset text paths** (e.g., spirals and waves) can be applied to any artistic text.

Drawing

- **Design inspiration**
  Use the Online tab to view video tutorials explaining how to use CraftArtist's tools and how to apply various creative techniques.

- **QuickShapes** (p. 159)
  QuickShapes work like intelligent clipart which can morph into a myriad of different shape variations. Even extremely complex shapes like spirals, stars, and webs are simple to draw.

- **Copy fills and effects between objects!** (p. 177)
  Use the **Format Painter** to copy fills and effects between objects.

- **Color and transparency control** (p. 217)
  Apply solid color or transparency to any drawn item's line or fill (or brush stroke) with the Color tab. The tab hosts color **swatches** from Digikits, an HSL color wheel (for custom color selection), and transparency slider. Use the **Fill Tool** to apply gradient, plasma, or mesh fills for exciting results—a gradient fill path lets you add or replace colors and/or transparency simultaneously for more subtle gradients.

- **Design your own custom color palettes with Color Palette Designer**
  For quick results, simply pick your base color and then choose from a range of related colors. You can add suggested colors automatically, or mix your own colors to create a new palette. (See *Creating custom palettes* in CraftArtist Help.)

- **Filter effects** (p. 143)
  Give your project items depth with Material Depth or soft edges with Feather Edge. Why not apply drop shadows with the **Shadow Tool**? All are easy to apply and sure to impress.

- **Astounding 3D lighting and surface effects** (p. 147)
  The Studio's Effects tab offers preset 3D effects (metals, elements, glass, stone, wood, and more) you can apply one or more effects, then customize by varying surface and source light properties.

Sharing

- **Share via website** (p. 247)
  Upload projects to Serif's digital craft community website, **www.daisytrail.com**. View layouts using powerful **zoom** technology, **comment** on, or **search** for any project by tag. Create public or private **groups** for like-minded crafters—great for making new friends! Take part in craft discussions in DaisyTrail's **forums**.

- **Email project images to friends and family**
  Send your project as Adobe PDF and the popular JPEG format—or simply email your *.craft file!

Installation

System requirements

Minimum:

- Windows-based PC with DVD drive and mouse

- Microsoft Windows® XP (32 bit), Windows® Vista, or Windows® 7 operating system

- 512MB RAM

- 266MB (recommended full install) free hard disk space (program only)*

- 1024 x 768 monitor resolution

* Does not include space requirements for Digikit collections and downloaded Digikits.

Additional disk resources and memory are required when editing large or complex documents.

 To enjoy the full benefit of brushes and their textures, you'll need a computer whose processor supports SSE. On brush selection, an on-screen message will indicate if your computer is non-SSE.

Optional:

- Windows-compatible printer

- TWAIN-compatible scanner and/or digital camera

- Pen (graphics) tablet

- Internet account and connection required for accessing downloadable DaisyTrail.com Digikits, online resources, and project upload

Installation procedure

- Insert your purchased DVD into your DVD drive.

  - If AutoPlay is enabled on the drive, this automatically starts the Setup Wizard. Follow the on-screen instructions for install.

    -or-

  - If AutoPlay is not enabled (or doesn't start the install automatically), run **setup.exe** from your DVD.

Getting started

2

Using the Startup Wizard

Once you have installed CraftArtist, you're ready to start crafting! By default, a **Serif CraftArtist** item is added to the **All Programs** submenu of the Windows **Start** menu.

Opening the Startup Wizard

- Use the Windows **Start** menu to open CraftArtist.

  -or-

- If CraftArtist is already running, on the **File** menu, click **New>New from Startup Wizard...**

The Startup Wizard offers different routes into the program:

Option	Allows you to...
Choose a Template	Create a CraftArtist Project (greeting card, scrapbook, photobook, etc.) based on a template. You can customize the layout to suit your needs by adding your own photos, text, and decorative items.
Blank Project	Create a new CraftArtist project from scratch.
Make & Do Project	Create physical projects (rather than electronic ones) such as greeting cards. Follow the written and video instructions step-by-step for beautiful cards you can pop in the post box!
Download Free Digikits	Access free to use Digikits hosted on DaisyTrail.
Visit DaisyTrail Shop	Buy Digikit Collections and individual Digikits on DaisyTrail.

Use the **Open** section to launch recently opened and saved CraftArtist projects (plus unopened projects). Hover over each entry for a quick preview before clicking!

The **Learn** section allows you to access online video tutorials hosted on DaisyTrail, as well as the DaisyTrail gallery and forums. The **CraftArtist User Guide** (PDF format) tells you all you need to know about CraftArtist.

Turning the Startup Wizard off and on

If you don't want the Startup Wizard to display every time you open CraftArtist, you can turn it off.

To turn off the Startup Wizard:

- In the lower-left corner of the Startup Wizard, click **Don't show this wizard again**.

    -or-

1. On the **Tools** menu, click **Options...**

2. In the **Options** dialog, under **Ease of Use**, clear the **Startup Wizard** check box.

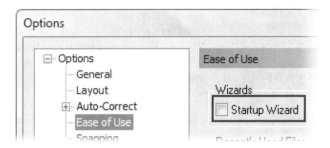

🔖 Both methods only turn the Startup Wizard off when you open CraftArtist. Once the program is open, you can still access the Startup Wizard by clicking **File>New>New from Startup Wizard**.

To turn the Startup Wizard back on:

1. On the **Tools** menu, click **Options...**

2. In the **Options** dialog, under **Ease of Use**, select the **Startup Wizard** check box.

    -or-

1. On the **File** menu, click **New>New from Startup Wizard**.

2. Click to clear the **Don't show this wizard again** box.

Understanding Craft Projects

CraftArtist is project based, and allows you to create **greeting cards**, **scrapbooks**, **photobooks**, **stationery**, **gift wrap**, and **party crafts** from project templates or from scratch. Your saved work can then be saved as a **Craft Project** (*.craft) file.

Template-based projects

The projects you can create depend on the product you've purchased and any installed Digikit you've downloaded and installed. As an example, the *Greeting Cards Digikit Collection* contains many Digikits, each packed with different layouts to make your Greeting Card project template. Similarly, the *Scrapbooks Digikit Collection* provides scrapbook layouts, the *Baby Photos Digikit Collection* provides baby-related layouts, etc.

The project types are as follows:

Greeting Cards

You can choose from greeting card layouts from your installed Digikits. Layout types include Side Fold, Tent Fold, Tri-Fold, Z-fold.

Scrapbooks

This project type is for typical 12" x 12" scrapbook pages.

The Digikit layouts are all designed for the creation of stunning scrapbooks.

Embellishments, materials for cutting, and textured backgrounds all contribute to great layouts.

Photobooks

Photobook layouts are packed with photo frames which automatically populate with your favorite hand-picked photos. Great for photo-rich wedding and baby albums!

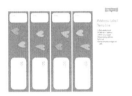

Stationery

Create your own personalized stationery including invitations, RSVPs, menus, thank you cards, and much more.

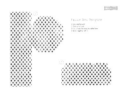

Gift Wrap

Diverse layouts are provided for gift wrap (Gift bags, boxes, and tags).

Party Crafts

Start celebrating with room, glass, and cupcake decorations, plus party masks, place cards, and table numbers!

Template-based projects are created from the Startup Wizard's **Choose a Template** option. (See *Starting from a template* on p. 21).

 Whichever layout you then select, you'll also get all other items from the Digikit added to the Content tabs in your workspace.

Blank projects

By starting from scratch, you can still create any of the above project types, but as simple **empty** page layouts.

4"x6" Folded   4.25"x5.5" Folded

5"x5" Folded   5"x7" Folded

By using the Digikit Browser (see p. 53), you can then choose any installed Digikit to pick items to base your project on. This gives you more flexibility in design.

Blank projects are created from the Startup Wizard's **Blank Project** option. (See *Starting projects from scratch* on p. 32).

Starting from a template

Digikits offer a selection of template layouts, backgrounds, frames, materials, letters, embellishments, brushes, swatches, and effects.

If you want to get started quickly, selecting a template will help you to create your first project in just a few easy steps.

There's no need to worry about your project paper sizes as your project will automatically scale to your printer's paper size.

You can also create original projects from scratch. See *Starting a project from scratch* on p. 32.

 Additional Digikits are available from the **www.daisytrail.com** website.

Choosing a layout

1. Launch CraftArtist, or click **File>New>New from Startup Wizard...**

2. In the Startup Wizard, click **Choose a Template.**

> If you've switched the Startup Wizard off, you can switch it on again. Click **Tools>Options**, select the **Ease of Use** option, and then select the **Startup Wizard** check box.

3. From the dialog's **Craft Projects** tab, select the type of project you want to create, e.g. Greeting Cards, Scrapbook Pages, PhotoBooks, etc.

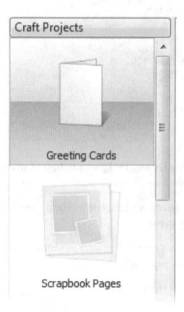

4. In the middle pane, scroll to review each layout; on hover over, each layout's thumbnail gives a visual indication of your printed project. You'll see the same set of layouts repeated for each installed Digikit in turn.

5. Click to select the layout.

MyCraft12 - Layout (60.0 pic x 30.0 pic)

6. Click **OK** to exit the dialog. The first page of the layout opens in the
    workspace, and all of the design items contained in the Digikit are
    added to the Content tabs at the left of the workspace.

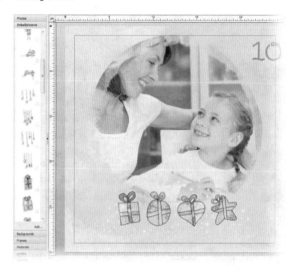

7. Running horizontally along the lower edge of the workspace, the **Pages** tab displays the pages you chose to add to your project.

   Click through the thumbnails to view these pages in the workspace and choose the page you want to work on first.

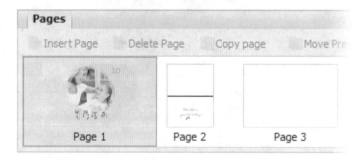

For fixed layouts such has greeting cards (above), your pages are added automatically. For other projects, you can insert, copy, move, and delete pages without constraint. (See *Adding, moving, and deleting pages* on p. 63.)

Adding your own photos

1. On the **Photos** tab, click **Add...**

2. In the **Open** dialog, browse to and select the photos you want to add to your project.

   - To select multiple adjacent files, press and hold down the **Shift** key, click the first file in the list, and then click the last file.

   - To select multiple non-adjacent files, press and hold down the **Ctrl** key, and then click to select.

3. Click **Open**. Your photos are added to the **Photos** tab.

4. To add a photo to your page, simply drag it from the **Photos** tab. You can drag directly onto the page, or onto an existing photo frame.

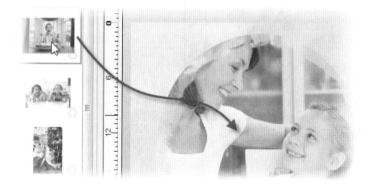

Adjusting and replacing framed photos

1. Select the framed photo, and then click the **Crop** button.

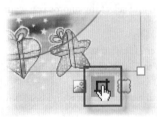

2. To rotate, or zoom into or out of the photo, click the buttons displayed at the right edge of the photo.

3. To pan the photo, click and drag on it.

4. To close the Crop window, click ⬑ **Back**, or click elsewhere on the page or pasteboard area.

To replace a photo:

- Drag a different photo onto a frame from the **Photos** tab.

  -or-

1. Select the framed photo you want to replace, then click the 🖼 **Select Cropped Object(s)** button that displays below it.

2. Click the 🖼 **Replace Photo** button on the Photo context toolbar.

3. Browse to and select the photo you want to add and click **Open**.

💡 You can preview a photo in a frame by dragging the photos over the frame (without releasing the mouse button).

Changing backgrounds

- From the Backgrounds tab, drag a different thumbnail onto your existing background.

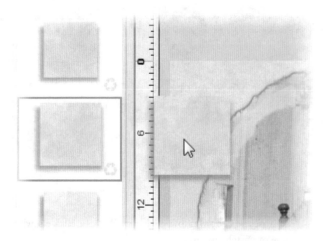

Sentiments

To insert a new sentiment:

1. To add a preset sentiment, select ▦ **Insert Sentiment** from the Pages context toolbar (ensure **Select** tool is enabled).

2. From the dialog, choose a sentiment category and then your sentiment from the right-hand pane.

3. Click **Insert**.

> ✎ For unwanted sentiments on your page, simply select with the **Select** tool and press **Delete**.

You can edit the sentiment as before to change age, dates, etc.

To edit an existing sentiment:

1. Open the Pages tab.

2. Select the page on which the sentiment is located.

3. Click in the sentiment text and edit the sentiment. Great for changing the age on a greeting card!

> You can save any text as a sentiment for later use, by clicking **Add as sentiment**, appearing under the text.

Adding letters and numbers

1. Open the **Letters** tab.

2. To add an individual letter or number, drag it from the tab onto your page.

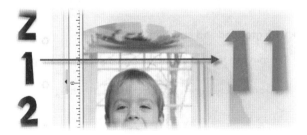

-or-

To add an entire word or phrase all at once, type it into the text box at

the bottom of the tab and click **Insert**. The word is added directly onto the page.

3. Use the Color tab to color the word or selected letters. Even add drop shadows using the Shadow tool.

To work with grouped and ungrouped letters:

- To **move** an individual letter or a group of letters, simply drag it.

- To **resize** a letter or group, select it, and then drag a corner handle.

- To **rotate** a letter or group, select it, and then drag its rotate handle.

- To **delete** a letter or group, select it and press the **Delete** key.

- To **group** letters, click and drag to draw a selection marquee around them. (To avoid selecting the object beneath the letters, hold down the **Alt** key as you drag.)

Release the mouse button and then click the 🔲 **Group** button.

- To **ungroup**, select the group and click the 🔲 **Ungroup** button.

Adding decorative items

1. In the Content tabs at the left of the workspace, open the **Embellishments** or the **Materials** tab.

2. Scroll the tab to find the item you want to add, and then drag it onto your page.

3. To move, resize, rotate, or delete an item, use the methods described above in Adding letters.

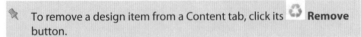

To remove a design item from a Content tab, click its **Remove** button.

Starting projects from scratch

If you decide to create your project from scratch, the first step is to select the page size and layout for your project.

Creating a new blank project

1. Launch CraftArtist, or click **File>New>New from Startup Wizard...**

2. In the Startup Wizard, click **Blank Project**.

If you've switched the Startup Wizard off, you can switch it on again. Click **Tools>Options**, select the **Ease of Use** option, and then select the **Startup Wizard** check box.

If the Startup Wizard is turned off, or you cancel the wizard, a new blank page will open of the type and size you last created.

Choosing page size and layout

When starting a blank project, you'll be able to set up your page size and layout initially, using standard or custom page sizes.

Using standard page sizes

1. From the **Page Setup** dialog, select your project type from the left-hand pane, e.g. Scrapbook Pages.

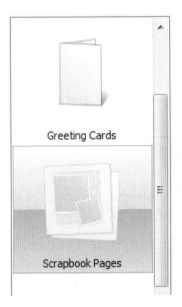

2. From the middle pane, navigate the categories and click on your chosen page layout.

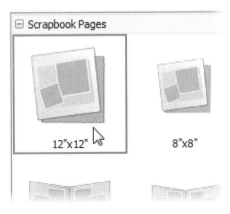

Page margins are represented on the page area by solid blue guides (Left, Top, Right, and Bottom).

3.   Click **OK** to accept the new dimensions. The updated settings are applied to the current project.

Instead of picking standard page sizes your project can be based on a custom page size instead.

Using custom page sizes

-   From the Page Setup dialog's middle pane, scroll down to the **Custom** option, and click it.

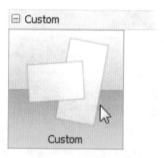

Custom

-   From the right-hand pane, edit the settings to create your custom page. You can also swap to a different layout for folded documents.

Paper	
Units	Inches
Paper Size	Custom size
Width	6.0 in
Height	6.0 in
Orientation	Landscape
Folding	
Type	None
Facing Pages	No
Margins	
Left	0.208 in
Top	0.208 in
Right	0.208 in
Bottom	0.208 in

To change your project's page setup at any time:

1.   On the Pages context toolbar, click 🗔 **Page Setup**.

2.   Select a project type and page layout as described above.

Changing page units

The width, height, and margins of your page (its printing dimensions) are shown in **page units**. You can change the unit without altering the page's actual dimensions.

- From the Page Setup dialog, choose different page **Units** in the right-hand pane.

   -or-

1.   In your workspace, right-click the ⌷ in ◿ box which intersects your horizontal and vertical rulers at the top-right of your workspace.

2.   From the flyout menu, select a different page unit.

> 🖈 The page size and margin settings are automatically saved with your project. Normally, they are also recorded as 'master settings,' which will be in effect the next time you start CraftArtist or create a new project. You can change which settings become master settings. For details, see *Recording master settings* in CraftArtist Help.

For projects created from templates, you won't need to worry about page size and layout as this is automatically set according to the template you've chosen (your design will scale at print time). However, you may still wish to access Page Setup for several reasons:

- You may want to quickly view your page size and layout to check your project settings.

- You may need to work to a set paper size, perhaps if you're printing professionally.

Choosing page backgrounds

1. In the **Digikit Browser,** you'll see installed Digikits, plus featured free and purchasable Digikits from the DaisyTrail.com shop. (See *Buying Digikits* on p. 57.) Select the Digikit you want to browse by clicking its thumbnail.

◢ My Digikits

Afternoon Tea   Modern Lace

2. Scroll to the **Backgrounds** category. You'll see the backgrounds available from the selected Digikit.

◢ Backgrounds

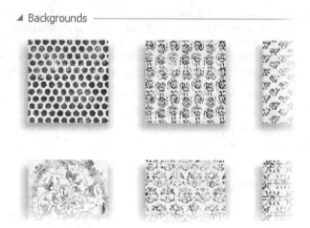

3. Click the background(s) that you want to use in your project.

-or-

To add all items from the Digikit, click **Add all items** .

 If you select an item from a featured free or purchasable Digikit—
the **Digikit Not Installed** dialog will display and you will be
prompted to visit the DaisyTrail.com shop. Once you've installed
your free or purchased Digikit, the item will be added to the
relevant Contents tab on selection. (See *Buying Digikits* on p. 57.)

In the Content tabs at the left of the workspace, the **Backgrounds** tab
displays the backgrounds you added to the project.

4. (Optional) Click 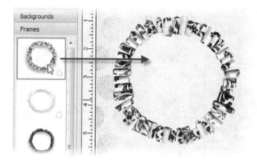 **Back to all Digikits** to add backgrounds from other Digikits.

5. Click **Done**.

6. Drag the background you want to use onto your page.

> 📌 To change the background, simply drag a new one onto the page.
>
> 📌 To remove a background from the **Backgrounds** tab, click its ♻ **Remove** button.

Adding photo frames

1. On the **Frames** tab, click **Add...**

2. The **Digikit Browser** opens to display frames, categorized by the name of the Digikit to which they belong. Scroll to the Digikit category you want to add frames from. You can add frames from more than one Digikit.

3. Click a frame to add it to your craft project, or click ⬤ **Add all items** to add them all. The selected frames are added to the **Frames** tab.

4. When you've finished selecting frames, click **Done**.

5. Drag a frame from the **Frames** tab onto your page.

Once the frame is added to the page, you can move, resize, and rotate it.

To remove a frame from the **Frames** tab, click its Remove button.

Adding photos

1. On the **Photos** tab, click **Add...**

2. In the **Open** dialog, browse to and select the photos you want to add.

   - To select multiple adjacent files, press and hold down the **Shift** key, click the first file in the list, and then click the last file.

   - To select multiple non-adjacent files, press and hold down the **Ctrl** key, and then click to select.

3. Click **Open**. Your photos are added to the **Photos** tab.

4. Drag a photo from the **Photos** tab and drop it onto a frame, or onto the page.

5. (Optional) You can adjust your photo inside its frame, or even replace it if required. For details, see Adjusting framed photos on p. 112.

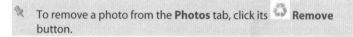

To remove a photo from the **Photos** tab, click its Remove button.

See also *Replacing and resizing photos* and *Fitting photos to frames* on p. 115 and p. 108, respectively.

Adding decorative items

1. On the **Embellishments** or **Materials** tab, click **Add...**

2. The **Digikit Browser** opens to display **Embellishments** or **Materials**, categorized according to the Digikit to which they belong. Select the category from which you want to add items. (You can add items from more than one Digikit.)

3. Click an item to add it to your craft project, or click **Add all items** to add them all.

In the workspace, the items you added are displayed in the relevant Contents tab.

4. When you've finished selecting items, click **Done**.

5. To add an item to your page, drag it from its tab.

6. Once an item is placed on the page, you can move, resize, and rotate it as required.

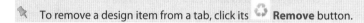 To remove a design item from a tab, click its ⟳ **Remove** button.

Adding letters

1. On the **Letters** tab, click **Add...**

2. The **Digikit Browser** opens to display letter sets, which are categorized by the name of the Digikit to which they belong. Scroll to the Digikit category you want to add letters from. You can add letters from more than one Digikit.

3. Click the letter set to add all letters to your craft project. They are added to the **Letters** tab.

4. When you've finished selecting your letter set, click **Done**.

5. To add an individual letter, number, or special character (such as an accent,) drag it from the tab directly onto your page.

To add an entire word or phrase all at once, type it into the text box at the bottom of the tab and click **Insert**.

 To remove a letter from the **Letters** tab, click its ⟳ **Remove** button.

You can now move, resize, rotate, and delete these letters individually, or you can work with them as a group by first clicking the **Group** button. (See *Grouping items* on p. 243.)

Adding text

1. On the Standard toolbar, click the **A** **Text** tool.

2. To create text at the default size, click on your page to set a text insertion point.

    -or-

    Click and drag on your page to set the size of the text insertion point.

3. To set text attributes (font, size, etc.) before typing: Make your selections on the Text context toolbar. (See Formatting text on p. 125.)

4. To set text color, set the Line/Fill swatches on the **Color** tab. (See Changing line and fill color on p. 219.)

5. Start typing.

> You can also create **Shape Text**, by typing directly inside a QuickShape or drawn shape. See Adding text on p. 120.

Creating brush strokes

1. On the Standard toolbar, click the **Brush** tool.

2. At the right of the workspace, open the **Brushes** tab and select a brush category from the upper drop-down list, and then a specific brush.

3. On the Brush context toolbar, set the brush stroke properties (width, opacity, smoothness, etc.).

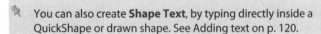

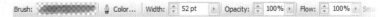

4. Drag a brush stroke across your page.

5. To create new brush strokes, repeat the click and drag process.

6. (Optional) Swap to a different brush on the Brushes tab for other brush effects, e.g. spray brushes for flowers, then continue painting.

7. When you have finished painting, to deselect the brush stroke press the Esc key.

Brushes used in the current project are added to the **Document** category of the **Brushes** tab.

For more on brushes, see *Adding brush strokes* on p. 205.

Adding Digikit brushes

The **Brushes** tab's **Digikit** category displays the brushes added from Digikits. If you've previously chosen to add all the items from a Digikit, a selection of brush strokes will be displayed in this category.

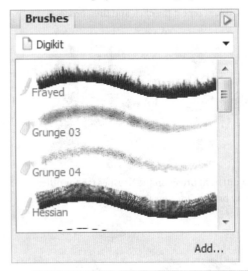

 Some Digikits don't contain brushes.

To add Digikit brushes:

1. On the **Pages Context** toolbar, click  **Add items from Digikits**. The **Digikit Browser** dialog opens.

2. Select the **Browse my items** tab.

3. Select the **Brushes** category from the left-hand category list.

4. Scroll the middle pane until you find a set of Digikit's brushes you like. Click to select the brush(es) you want to use.

◢ Indie Chic ——————————————————————————— Add all items

5. (Optional) Click  **Back to all Digikits** to add brushes from other Digikits.

6. Click **Done**.

Make & Do projects

Make & Do projects are a great excuse to get the scissors and glue out and try your hand at some 'real' project. These are typically cards for occasions or simply based on a theme.

To make your project easy to complete, CraftArtist suggests equipment and materials needed. You'll also be able to follow a step-by-step video along with written How To instructions.

CRAFTARTIST

PROJECT: Butterfly Card

Time to allow: 1 hour
Skill Level: Beginners

You will need:
A4/Letter card stock
glue
scissors
craft-knife
3D foam pads
glitter
ribbon
pencil
ruler
jewels
sequins

To make this project, just follow the step-by-step instructions. You can watch the video now or click here to start.

START ▶

Each Make & Do project is actually a *.craft file, containing all the instructions, examples, and embellishments you'll need. The embellishments can be printed and cut out to complete your project.

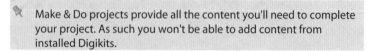

> Make & Do projects provide all the content you'll need to complete your project. As such you won't be able to add content from installed Digikits.

Starting a Make & Do Project

1. Launch CraftArtist, or click **File>New>New from Startup Wizard...**

2. In the Startup Wizard, click **Make & Do Project.**

> If you've switched the Startup Wizard off, you can switch it on again. Click **Tools>Options**, select the **Ease of Use** option, and then select the **Startup Wizard** check box.

3. From the dialog, choose a level which you feel most comfortable with—Beginner, Intermediate, or Advanced. Different Craft Projects will be offered for each level.

4. Select the project you want to make, then click **OK**.

5. Open the Pages tab, by clicking the ⬛⬛▲⬛ button at the bottom of your workspace.

6. Make your project by following the Start Page then Instructions page. Subsequent Print Template pages let you edit, print, and cutout embellishments for your project.

Opening and displaying projects

You can open an existing project from the Startup Wizard or the File menu. If you have more than one project open, you can switch between them using the **Window** menu or the document tabs.

Opening a recently opened project (via Startup Wizard)

1. From the Startup Wizard (at startup time or via **File>New...**), select your project from the Open section. The most recently opened project will be shown at the top of the list. To see a thumbnail preview of any project before opening, hover over its name in the list.

2. Click the file name to open it.

CraftArtist opens the file as a maximized currently active project.

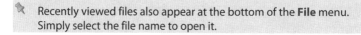
Recently viewed files also appear at the bottom of the **File** menu. Simply select the file name to open it.

Opening any project

1.   From the Startup Wizard (at startup time or via **File>New...**), click **Open....**

     -or-

     Choose **Open...** from the **File** menu (at any time).

2.   In the Open dialog, select the folder and file name.

3.   Click **Open** to open the desired project as a maximized document.

Browsing your projects

1.   Choose **Browse...** from the **File** menu.

2.   In the **Open Saved Work** dialog, in the **Documents** pane:

     • Use the **Folders** tab to browse your computer's folder structure and locate your projects.

          -or-

     • Use the **History** tab to view your most recently used projects.

3.   On the right, preview thumbnails of your saved projects are displayed.

     You can choose between **Thumbnails View** (displays thumbnails only), or **Details View** (displays thumbnails and information about the file—file size, creation date, and so on).

     Click a thumbnail, and then click **Open**.

Displaying projects

If you have multiple craft projects open at the same time, there are several ways to jump between them quickly.

Displaying a project from the Window menu:

- Select a project name from the **Window** menu.

  Unsaved projects are indicated with an asterisk.

  The currently active project is indicated with a check mark.

Displaying a project from the document tabs:

- In the upper left area of the workspace, click on an open project's tab to make it active. The file names of projects that are not active are grayed out.

Saving your work

The first time you save your work:

1. Click **Save**.

2. In the **Save As** dialog:

   - Type a file name.

   - Browse to and select the destination for your saved file.

   - Click **Save**.

On subsequent saves:

- To save the project under its current name, click the **Save** button (or use **Ctrl+S** on your keyboard). The existing project file is overwritten with your recent changes.

- To save the project under a different name, click **File>Save As...** to open the **Save As** dialog.

CraftArtist periodically autosaves your work to a temporary file, allowing you to recover as much as possible in the event of a system failure. You can set autosave frequency under the **General** option of the **Tools>Options...** dialog.

Craft projects are saved with a *.craft file extension.

Digikits

Browsing

The **Digikit Browser** provides access to your installed Digikits, and to featured free and purchasable Digikits from **daisytrail.com**. You can browse Digikits and preview the items they contain, before adding them to your workspace.

You can also use the search controls at the right of the dialog to narrow your search, or to find a specific item. There are two ways to browse Digikit items—by Digikit, or by item category.

Browsing Digikits

1. On the Pages context toolbar, click **Add items from Digikits**.

2. In the **Digikit Browser**, you'll see installed Digikits, plus featured free and purchasable Digikits from the DaisyTrail.com shop. (See *Buying Digikits* on p. 57.)

   Browse the Digikits in **My Digikits**, **Featured Free DaisyTrail.com Digikits** and **DaisyTrail.com Digikits** categories. Hover over your chosen Digikit to see a zoomed-in preview for further inspection, then click its thumbnail.

3. Scroll through the categories to browse items included in the Digikit.

4. (Optional) To narrow your search, filter items by clicking tag names (e.g., Flower) in the Categories section. (See *Applying a search filter* on p. 54.)

5. To browse another Digikit, click **Back to 'All Digikits'**.

Browsing items

1. In the **Digikit Browser** dialog, click the **Browse my items** tab. You'll see items belonging to installed Digikits, plus featured free and purchasable Digikits from the DaisyTrail.com shop. (See *Buying Digikits* on p. 57.)

2. On the left-hand side of the dialog, select an item category you want to browse, e.g., **Embellishments**.

3. The items are categorized further in the middle pane by the name of the Digikit to which they belong, e.g., Afternoon Tea. Scroll through to browse the items included in each Digikit. To make browsing easier, you can expand and collapse the Digikit categories to hide or reveal the items.

4. (Optional) To narrow your search, filter items by clicking tag names (e.g., Flower) in the Categories section. (See Applying a search filter.)

Applying a search filter

The filter searches preset and custom tags applied to all of the Digikits shown in the **Digikit Browser** (this includes Digikits you have installed, and Digikits available from the DaisyTrail.com shop). (See *Tagging* in CraftArtist Help.)

1. Click **Add items from Digikits**.

2. Click **Browse Digikits** or **Browse my items**, depending on which browsing method you prefer.

3. There are two methods by which you can apply search filters, and both can be used together to further narrow your search.

- Select a preset search tag from the drop-down menus.

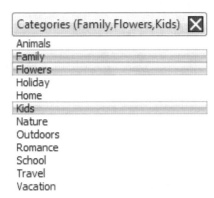

- Type the word or letter you want to search for in the **Search** text box, situated at the right of the dialog. This is useful for retrieving items with custom tags attached.

Ctrl-click to select more than one filter. Click ✕ to remove the filter(s).

If you've searched via the **Browse Digikits** tab, the Digikit containing the relevant items is displayed for you to select and browse further.

Painted Backyard

If you've searched via the **Browse my items** tab, click on each category, e.g., **Frames**, to reveal the relevant items.

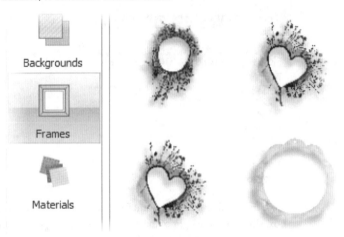

Adding items to your workspace

- To add items to your workspace via the **Browse Digikits** tab, select the Digikit you want to browse and then simply click the item you want to add.

- To add items to your workspace via the **Browse my items** tab, select the category you want to browse, and then simply click the item.

- To add all items from a selected Digikit, select the Digikit, and then click the **Add Digikit** button that displays in the lower-left corner of the dialog.

- To add all items in a category, click the Add all items button that displays in the upper-right corner of each category's thumbnail gallery.

If you select an item, or add all items, from a featured free or purchasable Digikit—the **Digikit Not Installed** dialog will display and you will be prompted to visit the DaisyTrail.com shop.

- To remove a specific item from your workspace, select the item and click the **Remove** button via the **Digikit Browser** or subsequently via the relevant Contents tab.

- To remove all items from your workspace, click the **Clear All Categories** button that displays in the lower-left corner of the dialog.

Buying Digikits

Buying Digikit collections

CraftArtist is supplied with at least one **Digikit Collection** for Baby Photos, Greeting Cards, Scrapbooks, or Wedding Day, depending on which product version you've bought. For any Digikit Collection you'll find an impressive selection of themed Digikits to choose from.

> You can also buy a range of DaisyTrail Digikit Collections.

To buy other Digikit Collections:

1. Launch CraftArtist, or click **File>New>New from Startup Wizard...**

2. In the Startup Wizard, click **Choose a Template.**

3. From the dialog's **Digikit Collections** tab, select the collection you wish to purchase.

4. In the middle pane, follow the instructions to purchase your new Digikit collection. You'll be taken to daisytrail.com to carry out your purchase.

Once you've installed the new Digikit collection, you'll see all of your newly purchased Digikits appear in the Digikits tab directly under the dialog's **Digikit Collections** tab.

Buying individual Digikits

You can also buy individual Digikits from the DaisyTrail shop. Provided that you have an internet connection, the **Digikit Browser** will automatically update to display the Digikits currently available for purchase from the website.

To buy a Digikit:

1. On the Pages context toolbar, click **Add items from Digikits**.

2. In the **Digikit Browser**, scroll to the **DaisyTrail.com Digikits** category.

3. Click the Digikit you want to buy and scroll through the categories to browse included items. You can also use the search controls on the right of the dialog to narrow the list of items, or search for a specific item. (See *Browsing* on p. 53.)

4. Click any item. The **Digikit Not Installed** dialog is displayed and provides a brief summary of the Digikit.

Camping

This Digikit is available to buy on DaisyTrail.com! If you would like to buy the Digikit, click Visit Shop below.

This pack contains:

- 34 embellishments
- 7 backgrounds
- 5 frames
- 14 materials
- 77 letters
- 4 layouts
- 10 brushes

Visit Shop   Close

5. Click **Visit Shop**. The daisytrail.com shop opens in your web browser for you to proceed with your purchase.

> If you've not already registered on daisytrail.com, you will have to register on the website.

If you don't want to immediately buy the Digikit, you can add the Digikit to a wishlist (click **Add to Wishlist**)—a list of items you want to have. You can return at a later date to make your purchase.

Downloading free Digikits

DaisyTrail.com offers a featured free Digikit for you to download to use in your projects.

Provided that you have an internet connection, the **Digikit Browser** will automatically update to display the Digikits currently available for free download. Digikits made available for free download are often themed according to current or upcoming seasons, celebrations, public holidays, and vacations—Independence Day, Mother's Day, Father's Day, Easter, Christmas, Halloween, and so on.

To download a free Digikit:

1. On the Pages context toolbar, **Add items from Digikits**.

2. In the **Digikit Browser**, scroll to the **Featured Free DaisyTrail.com Digikits** category.

3. Click the Digikit you want to download and scroll through the categories to browse included items. You can also use the search controls on the right of the dialog to narrow the list of items, or search for a specific item. (See *Browsing* on p. 53.)

4. Click any item. The **Digikit Not Installed** dialog is displayed and provides a brief summary of the Digikit.

5. Click **Download**. DaisyTrail.com opens in your web browser for you to proceed with your free download.

If you've not already registered on DaisyTrail.com, you will have to register on the website.

Pages and design aids

Adding, moving and deleting pages

All pages in your project are displayed in the Pages tab, which can be expanded from the bottom of your workspace.

To expand the Pages tab:

- Click on the ▬▬▲▬▬ button at the bottom of the workspace. Click the button again to collapse the tab.

Depending on your project, the way you work with multiple pages will vary.

For **scrapbooks**, **photobooks**, **stationery**, and **gift wrap**:

- Projects can consist of a single page, or a series of pages made up of various pre-defined layouts. You can add pages to your project designs by adding your own blank pages.

For **greeting cards** only:

- Cards use a "fixed" multiple page layout, with a back and front page and double inside pages. Due to the nature of folded cards, further pages cannot be added.

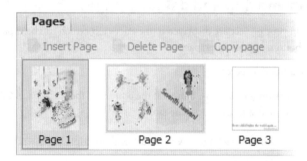

Adding pre-designed layouts

CraftArtist offers a range of pre-designed layouts within each Digikit which you use as the basis of your new page. By customizing each layout further, you can quickly create your own professional looking designs.

- Click the **Insert Page** icon in the Pages tab to access your installed Digikits and their layouts. Once you've selected a layout from the categorized pane, click **OK**.

  The layout is added as a new page as the last page in your project.

You can replace any page with a different layout by selecting the page first and simply dragging the layout from the Layouts tab onto it.

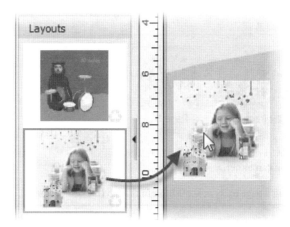

Adding blank pages

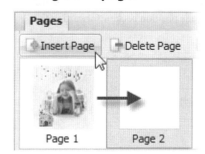

If you don't plan to work from a pre-designed layout, you can add blank pages from the Pages tab.

The new page is added after the currently selected page.

To add a new page:

1. On the **Pages** tab, select the page after which your new page will be added.

2. Click Insert Page. The new page is created and becomes the currently active page.

   -or-

   If on the last page, click the ▶ **Next Page** button on the HintLine toolbar and use the Page Manager's **Insert Page** tab.

Moving pages

From the **Pages** tab, you can either:

- Click and drag a page to its new position in the tab (illustrated above).

  -or-

- Select a page selected and click ⬚ **Move Previous** or ⬚ **Move Next**. The selected page jumps one position back or forward in the page order.

Deleting a selected page

On the **Pages** tab, select a page and click ⬚ **Delete Page**, or right-click on the page and click **Delete**.

Copying pages

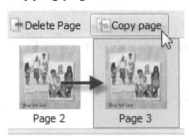

Use the **Copy page** button to base your new page on an existing page. Page items are copied across to the new page.

1. On the **Pages** tab, select the page you want to copy.

2. Click  **Copy Page** to create an identical copy immediately after the selected page.

Navigating pages

You can use the horizontal and vertical scroll bars to scroll the page and pasteboard area.

The Pages tab and HintLine toolbar provide additional controls to let you navigate between pages.

Navigating with the Pages tab

Once you have added pages, use the Pages tab to quickly navigate between pages.

1. To expand the **Pages** tab, click on the ▬▬▲▬▬ button at the bottom of the workspace.

   (Click the button again to collapse the tab.)

2. To view a specific page, simply select its thumbnail.

You can also use the ◀ ▶ page controls on the HintLine toolbar to navigate your pages. For details, see CraftArtist Help.

Panning and zooming

Use panning to move around zoomed-in areas of your project. A variety of tools and magnifying options are available for zooming into and out of your page.

The **Pan** and **Zoom** tools are located on the HintLine toolbar at the lower-right of the workspace.

Panning

Click the 🖑 **Pan Tool** and then click and drag on the page to reposition it in the window.

 If you're using a wheel mouse, you can hold down the middle button and drag anywhere on the page to reposition it in the window.

Zooming

The Zoom tools let you view and/or edit the page at different levels of detail.

You can zoom in/out in increments, or by a user-defined or preset amount.

- **60%** **Current Zoom:** Displays the current zoom percentage, with 100% representing an actual-size page. Click on the value to select a preset zoom from a pop-up menu, or type over the value for a custom zoom percentage.

- ⊖ **Zoom Out:** Click to decrease the current zoom percentage with each click.

- ⊕ **Zoom In:** Click to increase the current zoom percentage with each click.

- 🔍 **Zoom Tool:** Click the tool and then drag out a rectangular selection marquee on the page to define a region to zoom in to. The zoom percentage adjusts accordingly, fitting the designated region into the window.

- To zoom out, hold down the **Shift** key when dragging or just right-click on the page. You can also pan around a zoomed-in page while the **Ctrl** key is pressed. To zoom to the currently selected item, choose **Selection** from the **View** menu.

- **Fit Page:** Click to adjust the zoom percentage so the entire page area is displayed in the window.

> 💡 If you're using a wheel mouse, you can scroll the wheel forward or back to move up or down the page, or move horizontally left or right by using the Shift key and scrolling together. Try combining the Ctrl key and scrolling up or down for immediate in/out zoom control.

Using design aids

A number of tools are provided on the **HintLine toolbar** (at the bottom of the workspace) to assist you as you design. Typically the tools can be switched on or off as you go.

Rotating your canvas

Rotating your canvas helps you to maintain natural flow when drawing freeform lines, curves, or brush strokes, where the artist uses the wrist as a pivot (especially when using a pen tablet). If you rotate the canvas by a chosen angle then the drawing becomes easier—taking advantage of the natural arc of the drawing hand.

The previous example illustrates how grass-like brush strokes can be added to a canvas once it has been rotated 30°!

To rotate your canvas:

Either:

1. Click the **Rotate Canvas** button (don't click the down arrow).

2. Hover over your workspace until you see the cursor, then click and drag to rotate the canvas clockwise or counter-clockwise.

3. Once you're happy with the degree of rotation, release the mouse button to reposition the canvas.

-or-

- Click the down arrow on the **Rotate Canvas** button and choose a preset angle from the drop-down list.

> You can also select an item and then choose **To Item** from the **Rotate Canvas** drop-down list. The canvas adjusts so that the item is positioned square to the X and Y axes.

To reset your canvas:

- With the button enabled, double-click anywhere on the canvas to reset.

Applying the Rule of Thirds

Traditionally a technique used in photography, the **Rule of Thirds** grid can also be applied to CraftArtist projects to help you with page composition.

By aligning items to intersecting horizontal and vertical lines (rather than just centering items on the page) you can create greater visual interest.

When a grid is applied to your page the displayed context toolbar lets you alter the grid's color and opacity. You can also add more grids, delete, and reset a grid. (See CraftArtist Help.)

 The grid is actually an overlay which appears as an 'Overlay Layer' in the Layers tab.

To apply a Rule of Thirds grid:

1. Click **Rule of Thirds** on the HintLine toolbar. A blue grid is overlaid over your page.

2. (Optional) Drag a corner or edge handle to resize the grid; reposition the grid by dragging. Use over selected items (instead of the entire page) depending on what you're currently working on.

3. Place embellishments, photos, or cut materials onto any of the intersecting blue lines.

If at any point the **Rule of Thirds** grid becomes deselected, simply click the **Rule of Thirds** button again to reselect it.

Isolating items

For focused editing, CraftArtist provides the **Solo mode**. This allows you to temporarily isolate selected item(s), such as embellishments or photos, on the page that you are currently designing (all unselected objects disappear!). In doing so, you avoid having to move objects to other layers or lock object unnecessarily.

The selected balloon (selection shown in blue) can be isolated for detailed painting with a red brush.

- Select the item(s), then click  **Solo Mode**. Click the button again to return to normal editing mode.

Clipping items

Clipped mode cuts off (clips) items that hang over the edge of your canvas, and which would otherwise display on your gray pasteboard area. The option is turned on by default, but you can view your overlapping items unclipped if required.

To turn off Clipped mode:

- Disable the **Clipped Mode** button on the **HintLine** toolbar. Any overlapping items will then display in full. Click the button again to return to **Clipped** mode.

Working with photos

Adding and positioning your photos

You can use the following methods to add photos to your project:

- Use the **Photos** tab to store photos that you want to use in your project. You can then drag them onto the page as you need them, or use AutoFlow (p. 109) to quickly add them to frames you have already placed on your page.

- Use the Photo button on the Standard toolbar to add individual images directly to the page.

> Use the first method if you want to add multiple photos to your project all at once, or if you want to add your photos to photo frames.
>
> Use the second method if you want to add photos to your page individually, or if you want to add your own embellishments to your layout.

Adding photos to the Photos tab

1. In the Contents tabs at the left of the workspace, click the **Photos** tab to open it. At the bottom of the tab, click **Add...**

2. In the **Open** dialog, browse to and select the photos you want to add to your project.

    *   To select multiple adjacent files, press and hold down the **Shift** key, click the first file in the list, and then click the last file.

    *   To select multiple non-adjacent files, press and hold down the **Ctrl** key, and then click to select.

3. Click **Open**. Your photos are added to the **Photos** tab.

Adding photos to the page

To add a photo from the Photos tab:

There are several ways to add photos to your page:

- Drag a photo from the **Photos** tab directly onto the page, or onto a photo frame. (See *Adding photo frames* on p. 103.)

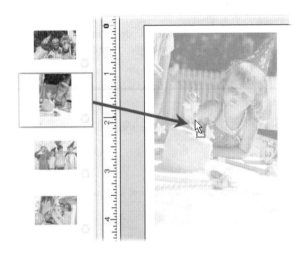

- Click **AutoFlow** to sequentially populate a series of photo frames with photos from the **Photos** tab. (See *Using AutoFlow* on p. 109.)

- Replace the contents of a photo frame by dragging a new photo onto the frame.

  On the **Photos** tab, framed and unframed photos added to your project are denoted with a ⊘ check mark icon. This lets you quickly and easily identify photos used in your project.

To add a photo from the Standard toolbar:

1. On the Standard toolbar, click **Photo**.

   -or-

   On the **Insert** menu, click **Photo>From File...**

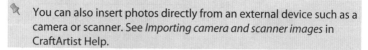

> You can also insert photos directly from an external device such as a camera or scanner. See *Importing camera and scanner images* in CraftArtist Help.

2. In the **Open** dialog, browse to and select the photo you want to add, and then click **Open**.

3. To insert the photo at default size, simply click the mouse.

   -or-

   To set the size of the photo, drag out a region and release the mouse button.

To add a photo by drag-and-drop:

- Drag and drop an image file or preview thumbnail into CraftArtist from Windows Explorer into the current workspace.

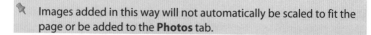

> Images added in this way will not automatically be scaled to fit the page or be added to the **Photos** tab.

Moving photos

1. Select the photo(s) with the ![Select tool cursor] **Select** tool.

2. Click inside the photo (not on a handle), hold down the left mouse button, and then drag to a new location.

    (Note that the cursor changes to a ![Move cursor] Move cursor.)

    -or-

    Click and drag the photo's ![Move button] **Move** button.

Replacing, resizing, and deleting photos

Once you've placed a photo on your page, you can replace, resize, or delete it as required.

Replacing photos

1. On the Standard toolbar, click the ![Select tool] **Select** tool, and then click to select the photo you want to replace.

2. On the Photo context toolbar, click ![Replace Photo icon] **Replace Photo**.

3. In the **Open** dialog, browse to and select the photo you want to add, and then click **Open**.

    The image is replaced.

When you replace a photo in this way, the aspect ratio of the original photo is used. This is fine if both of your images are the same aspect ratio. However, if your photos are of different dimensions, then it is better to delete the original image and add the new one.

To replace a framed photo:

- Drag a different photo onto the frame from the **Photos** tab, or use **AutoFlow** to automatically replace the contents of multiple frames in a single step. (See *Fitting photos to frames* on p. 103.)

Resizing photos

1. Select the photo with the  Select tool.

2. To resize the photo, drag a corner handle.

The photo's aspect ratio is preserved. To allow free resizing to any aspect ratio, hold down the **Shift** key while dragging.

Deleting photos

*   To remove a photo from the page, select the photo and press the **Delete** key.

*   To remove a photo from the **Photos** tab, click its ♻ **Recycle** button.

> For information on deleting framed photos, see *Deleting frames and framed photos* on p. 115.

Cropping your photos

CraftArtist includes the **Crop Tool** for cropping objects and photos on the page. The Crop context toolbar also provides a Rule of Thirds grid to help you with your photo composition (see p. 86).

> For information on working with framed photos, see *Fitting photos to frames* on p. 108.

Cropping a photo

1. Select a photo and then on the Standard toolbar, click the ▭ **Crop Tool**.

2. Click and drag an edge or corner handle towards the center of the photo.

Using the Rule of Thirds

1. Select your photo and click the  **Crop Tool**.

2. On the Crop context toolbar, click **Show/Hide Thirds Grid**.

3. A 3 x 3 grid is superimposed on top of the photo.

4. Drag an edge handle to crop the photo. The grid repositions itself on release.

5. To zoom into or out of the image, use the Zoom tools displayed to the right of the photo.

Click and drag on the cropped photo to pan the image.

For best results, aim to position your main subject of interest at a point where any two gridlines intersect.

Retouching photos

When you select a photo on the page, the Photo context toolbar displays.

In addition to replacing photos, this toolbar lets you quickly remove red eye, adjust brightness and contrast, apply auto level and auto contrast adjustments, and access PhotoLab (p. 89) and Cutout Studio (p. 97). You can use these tools on unframed and framed photos.

You can also convert unframed photos to "frameless" frames. (See *Converting photos to frames* on p. 116.)

Applying PhotoLab filters

PhotoLab is a dedicated studio environment that lets you apply adjustment and effect filters to photos, individually or in combination.

PhotoLab offers the following key features:

- **Adjustment filters**
  Apply tonal, color, lens, and sharpening filters.

- **Effect filters**
  Apply distortion, blur, stylistic, noise, render, artistic, and various other effects.

- **Retouching filters**
  Apply red-eye and spot repair correction.

- **Non-destructive operation**
  All filters are applied without affecting the original photo, and can be edited at any point in the future.

- **Powerful filter combinations**
  Create combinations of mixed adjustment, retouching, and effect filters for savable workflows.

- **Selective masking**
  Apply filters to selected regions using masks.

- **Save and manage favorites**
  Save filter combinations to a handy **Favorites** tab.

- **Viewing controls**
  Compare before-and-after previews, with dual- and split-screen controls. Use pan and zoom control for moving around your photo.

- **Locking controls**
  Protect your applied filters from accidental change, then optionally apply them to other images on selection.

PhotoLab includes filter tabs, a main toolbar, and an applied filter stack around a central workspace.

Photos present in your project display in the **Images** tab.

- If you can't see the **Images** tab, simply click the ▲ button at the bottom of the dialog.

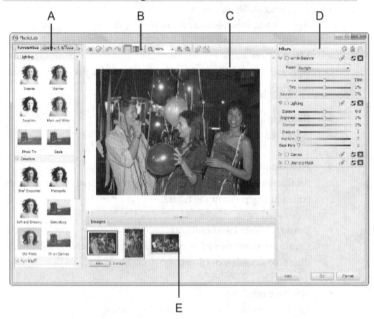

A	-	Filter tabs	D	-	Filter stack
B	-	Main toolbar	E	-	Images tab
C	-	Main workspace			

To launch PhotoLab:

1. Select the picture that you want to apply a filter to.

2. Click  **PhotoLab** on the context toolbar.

Using the images tab

Pictures present in your publication will show in the **Images** tab (**E** in the previous screenshot), if the tab is expanded. You can show or hide the tab by clicking the ▬▬▬▬ button at the bottom of your workspace.

To search publication images:

1. Click the Filter button on the **Images** tab.

2. Select and define a minimum and maximum size, if required.

3. Select or deselect RGB, CMYK and Grayscale to show only images in these color modes.

4. Click **OK**.

The **Images** tab displays only images which comply to the criteria set above.

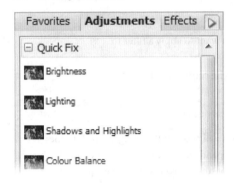

Filters are stored in the **Favorites**, **Adjustments**, and **Effects** filter tabs, and are grouped into categories.

For example, the **Adjustments** tab provides the **Quick Fix** and **Pro Edit** categories, while the **Effects** tab offers a wide range of creative effect categories.

On the **Favorites** tab, you'll find a selection of presets created with individual and combined filters. You can add your own custom filters to the **Favorites** tab. (See *Saving Favorites* on p. 96.)

When you apply a filter from one of these tabs, it is temporarily added to the **Trial Zone** that displays beneath the filter stack. This lets you preview and adjust filters before applying them.

Applying filters

1. Select the photo you want to work on. (If the photo is framed, select it and click ![icon] **Select Cropped Object**.)

2. Click ![icon] **PhotoLab** on the Photo context toolbar.

3. For ease of use, when you open PhotoLab, the **Filters** stack on the right contains some commonly-used filters (such as **White Balance** and **Lighting**). These filters are disabled by default.

To apply one of the default filters, click its ☐ **Enable/Disable** control to enable it, and then adjust the filter settings by dragging the sliders.

To disable, reset, and delete a filter, see below.

To add a new filter:

1. Browse the filter thumbnails displayed on the **Favorites**, **Adjustments**, and **Effects** tabs, and click the one you want to apply.

    The selected filter is added to the **Trial Zone**, and the main window shows a preview of your photo with the filter applied.

    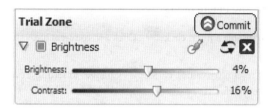

2. Experiment with the filter settings in the **Trial Zone**—you can drag the sliders, or enter values directly—to suit your requirements. (Note that some filters also offer check boxes, drop-down menus, and additional advanced controls.)

3. (Optional) To replace the trial filter, click a different thumbnail.

    Selecting a new filter always replaces the current filter in the trial zone.

4. To apply the filter, click 🅰 **Commit** to add it to the **Filters** stack.

5. (Optional):

    *   Repeat steps 1 to 4 to add more filters to the **Filters** stack.

        Filters are applied to a photo cumulatively, in the order in which they are added to the **Filters** stack. The most recently added filter always appears at the bottom of the stack. (See To reorder filters, below.)

- Disable, reset, and/or delete filters in the **Filters** stack. (See below.)

- Use zoom in/out buttons or a percentage magnification for detailed work.

- Use the retouch tools to fix red eye and remove blemishes. (See Retouching, below.)

6. To apply all filters in the **Filters** stack and close PhotoLab, click ✅ **OK**.

To disable, reset, and delete filters:

- To disable a filter, click 🔲 . Click 🔳 to re-enable.

- To reset filter values, click ↩ . Changes to settings revert to the filter's defaults.

- To delete a filter, click ❌ .

To reorder filters:

- Drag and drop your filter into any position in the stack. A dotted line indicates the new position in which the entry will be placed on mouse release.

To add a filter directly (without trialling):

- Click 🔧 **Add Quick Filter** at the top of the **Filters** stack and choose a filter from the flyout categories. The filter is applied directly to the stack without being added to the **Trial Zone**.

Retouching

PhotoLab's main toolbar provides some useful retouching tools. These are commonly used to correct photos before applying color correction and effects.

- **Red-eye tool**, to remove red eye from a human subject.

- **Spot-repair tool**, to remove blemishes from human skin and material surfaces.

For instructions on using the retouching tools, see CraftArtist Help.

Selective masking

You may sometimes want to apply a filter to selected regions of a photo, rather than to the entire photo. In PhotoLab, you can do this by using a "mask" to define these region(s).

You can apply a mask:

- To the areas to which you want to apply the filter.

  - or-

- To the areas you want to protect from the filter.

To apply a mask:

1. From the **Mask** drop-down menu, select **New Mask**.

2. In the **Mask Brush** pane, select the **Add Region** tool.

3. Adjust the settings to suit your requirements. For example, adjust **Brush Size** to paint larger or more intricate regions.

4. In the **Mode** drop-down menu, choose one of the following options:

    - **Select:** Choose this if you want to apply the filter only to the regions you paint. This is the default setting.

    - **Protect:** Choose this if you want to apply the filter to all areas of the photo, *except* for those that you paint.

5. Using the circular cursor, paint the regions to be masked (selected areas are painted in green; protected areas in red).

    If you've not been as accurate as you'd like while painting, click  **Remove Regions** then paint over the unwanted painted regions.

6. Click ✔ to save your mask changes, or ✖ to cancel.

You can create additional masks for the same filter, as above, and then choose between them. You can only apply one mask at any one time. By using the Mask menu's **New From>** option you can also base your new mask on an existing mask, which may be applied to the current filter or to any other filter in the stack. This is useful when working with **Favorites** filters that contain multiple adjustments.

To edit a mask:

- Expand the drop-down 🖊 Mask menu and select the mask you want to edit. Click **Edit Mask**.

Saving favorites

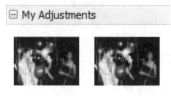

☐ My Adjustments

Dark pencil   Sepia pencil

You can save specific filter settings, or combinations of filters, as favorites for future use.

PhotoLab stores all your favorites together in the **Favorites** tab. You can even create your own categories (e.g. My Adjustments) within the tab.

To save and manage favorites:

1.   Click  **Save Filter**.

2.   In the dialog, type a name for your filter and choose the category in which to save it. (Click ▭ to create a new category.)

3.   (Optional) To organize your favorites into user-defined categories, click the ▷ **Tab Menu** button and choose **Manage Favorites**.

Using Cutout Studio

CraftArtist includes **Cutout Studio**, a powerful integrated solution for separating objects from their backgrounds. Whether you're discarding or replacing a photo background, or isolating a section of an image to use in your layout, Cutout Studio lets you create eye-catching pictures quickly and easily.

Opening Cutout Studio

1.   Select the photo you want to work with.

2.   On the Photo context toolbar, click ✎ **Cutout Studio**.

3.   Follow the instructions outlined below.

> 💡 You'll find detailed instructions in the **Help** tab at the right of the Cutout Studio window.

Choosing your approach

The approach you take depends on your photo content.

Discard Brush Tool

- If your subject of interest is placed against a simple, uniform background (sky, a wall, etc.), it's easier and quicker to **select and discard** the background.

Keep Brush Tool

- If the subject of interest is surrounded by a background consisting of complex colors or patterns (such as trees or buildings), it's easier to **select and keep the subject.**

Selecting areas to discard or keep

To select areas to discard or keep:

1. Click the  **Discard Tool** or the **Keep Tool**.

2. On the horizontal toolbar, select a brush size.

3. (Optional) To adjust the degree of precision with which areas are selected, select the **Grow Tolerance** check box and adjust the value.

4. Click and drag on the image to mark the areas you want to discard/keep. As you do so, CraftArtist locates similar adjoining areas and includes them in your selection.

5. Repeat the click and drag process until your selection area is complete.

6.　As you paint your image, you can view your progress using the buttons on the left toolbar.

- **Show original:** The default view mode. The image is shown in its original form.

- **Show tinted:** Areas marked to be kept are shown with a green tint; areas to be discarded are shown with a red tint.

- **Show transparent:** Areas marked for discarding are not shown. By default, these areas are replaced with a checkerboard background indicating transparency.

Choosing an output type

On the **Output Settings** tab, the **Output Type** drop-down list provides two output format options, **Alpha-edged bitmap**, and **Vector-cropped bitmap**. The format you choose depends on what you want to do with your resulting image.

General recommendations

Choose alpha-edged bitmap if you want to blend your cutout image into another image or background, or if your subject has poorly defined edges. Choose vector-cropped bitmap if you want to place your cutout image onto a plain or transparent background, or if your subject has more well-defined edges. (For more details on these output formats see CraftArtist Help.)

To create an alpha-edged bitmap:

1.　On the **Output Settings** tab, in the **Output Type** drop-down list, select **Alpha-edged Bitmap**.

2.　(Optional)

- Drag the **Width** slider to set the area of the image that is to be faded into the background. (Use a lower **Width** setting for small images, or those with intricate edges; use a higher setting for large images, or those with 'cleaner' edges.)

- Drag the **Blur** slider to smooth out the cutout edge.

3. To preview the cutout area, click **Preview**.

4. (Optional) Use the touch-up tools to further refine the cutout area (alpha-edged bitmaps only). (See *Refining the cutout area* on p. 100.)

5. To complete the cutout and return to the CraftArtist workspace, click **OK**.

To create a vector-cropped bitmap:

1. On the **Output Settings** tab, in the **Output Type** drop-down list, select **Vector-cropped Bitmap**.

2. (Optional)

    • Drag the **Feather** slider to adjust the softening effect around the edge of the cutout. This can improve the appearance of your image.

    • Drag the **Smoothness** slider to smooth out the cutout edge.

    • Drag the **Inflate** slider to adjust the cutout outline, moving it inward or outward.

> The **Inflate** adjustment is particularly useful if the edges of the subject include hair or fur, which usually also incorporate some of the background color.

3. To preview the cutout area, click **Preview**.

4. To complete the cutout and return to the CraftArtist workspace, click **OK**.

Refining the cutout area (alpha-edged bitmaps only)

1. On the **Output Setting** tab, click the **Preview** button. (You can use this button to check your cutout as you work.)

2. On the left toolbar, click the **Restore Touch-up Tool** or **Erase Touch-up Tool**.

3. Paint the areas for restoring or erasing as you would with the brush tools.

4. (Optional) To increase or decrease the opacity of the restored or erased areas, drag the **Hardness** slider (located on the horizontal toolbar).

    - Higher values will result in more pixels being erased, producing a more defined edge.

    - Lower values will produce a softer, more blended edge.

5. To complete the cutout and return to the CraftArtist workspace, click **OK**.

Editing the cutout area

If you've missed a portion of the photo intended to be discarded (or just removed too much), you can redefine the cutout area at any time.

To edit a cutout (alpha-edged bitmaps only):

1. Select your photo and on the Photo context toolbar, click **Cutout Studio**. The existing cutout area is displayed.

2. Fine-tune your selection as described above.

To edit a cutout (vector-cropped bitmaps only):

1. Select your photo and on the floating toolbar, click **Select Cropped Object(s)**.

2. On the Photo context toolbar, click **Cutout Studio**. The existing cutout area is displayed.

3. Fine-tune your selection as described above.

Adding photos
to frames

Adding photo frames to your project

CraftArtist Digikits include a wide selection of photo frames that you can add to your page. Once you've placed a frame on your page, simply drag a photo onto it—CraftArtist automatically fits the photo to the frame. All frames can be moved, resized, and rotated on the page.

Adding frames to the Frames tab

1. In the Content tabs at the left of the workspace, click the **Frames** tab to open it.

2. At the bottom of the **Frames** tab, click **Add...**

3. The **Digikit Browser** opens to display available frames, categorized by Digikit. Scroll to the Digikit from which you want to add frames. You can add frames from more than one Digikit.

4. Click a frame to add it to your craft project, or click **Add all items** to add them all.

    The selected frames are added to the **Frames** tab.

5. Click **Done** to close the **Digikit Browser**.

Once the frame is added to the page, you can move, resize, and rotate it.

To remove a frame from the **Frames** tab, click its ♻ **Remove** button.

Adding frames to the page

1.   Drag a frame from the **Frames** tab onto your page.

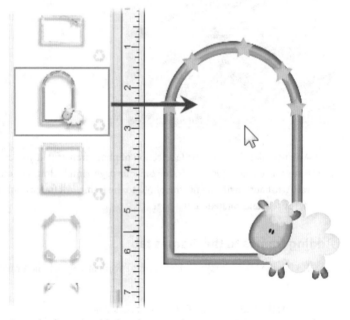

2.   Once the frame is added to the page, there are various ways to work with it.

- To resize the frame, drag a corner handle.

- To rotate the frame, drag the Rotate handle.

3. To add a photo to a frame, drag it from the **Photos** tab and drop it onto a frame.

   -or-

   Click **AutoFlow** to sequentially populate a series of photo frames with photos from the **Photos** tab. (See *Fitting photos to frames* on p. 108.)

Adding frames to existing photos

If you've already added a photo to your page, you can easily add a frame to it.

To add a frame to an existing photo:

- Drag a frame from the **Frames** tab and drop it onto the photo. CraftArtist fits the photo to the frame automatically.

To preview a frame:

- Drag a frame from the **Frames** tab and hover over the photo without releasing the mouse button. The photo is displayed the frame.

- To apply the frame, release the mouse button.
  - or -

  To select a different frame, drop the currently selected frame back onto the **Frames** tab, then drag a new frame onto your photo.

Fitting photos to frames

Once you have added your photos to the **Photos** tab, you can frame them on the page—manually by clicking and dragging, or automatically using **AutoFlow**. CraftArtist lets you rotate, zoom, and pan your framed photos inside their frames. You can even crop a framed photo and adjust its frame to follow suit!

You can also convert photos so that they sit inside "frameless" frames. Once converted, these frames function exactly like the decorative frames you've added from the **Frames** tab. (See *Converting photos to frames* on p. 116.)

Adding individual photos to frames

1. Add your photo(s) to the **Photos** tab. (See *Adding photos to the Photos tab* on p. 78.)

2. Add a frame to your page. (See *Adding frames to your project* on p. 105.)

3. Drag a photo from the **Photos** tab and drop it onto the frame. CraftArtist fits the photo to the frame automatically.

On the **Photos** tab, photos added to your craft project are denoted with a ✓ check mark icon.

Using AutoFlow

1. Add your photo(s) to the **Photos** tab. (See *Adding photos to the Photos tab* on p. 78.)

2. Add a frame to your page. (See *Adding frames to your project* on p. 105.)

3. On the **Photos** tab, click **AutoFlow** to automatically populate multiple photo frames.

4. The **AutoFlow Photos Into Frames** dialog opens, offering various options for filling your frames. For example, you can choose to replace existing photos in frames; randomize photo order; insert new pages to accommodate extra photos, and so on.

    Select any options you want to apply and click **OK**.

    - Frames are filled sequentially, from back to front in the **Z-order** (see *Ordering items* on p. 241).

        This means that if you haven't rearranged your frames (using the **Arrange** tab or the **Arrange>Order Items...** menu), they will be filled in the order in which you added them to your page.

    - By default, photos are placed in available frames in the order they appear on the **Photos** tab (unless you selected the **Randomize photo order** fill option).

5. If you have more frames than photos, or vice versa, a dialog will display.

    - If you have more frames than photos: Delete the unused frames, or add more photos and then drag them from the **Photos** tab and drop them onto the frames.

    - If you have more photos than frames: Add more frames to your page, and then drag the photos from the **Photos** tab and drop them onto the frames.

On the **Photos** tab, photos added to your page(s) are denoted with a check mark.

Cropping framed photos

1. Select the framed photo with the ![Select tool icon] **Select** tool.

2. Click ![Crop icon] **Crop**.

3. Drag the handles to crop the photo.

2.656 in

2.623 in

(See also *Cropping photos* on p. 85.)

4. Click ![Back icon] **Back** to return to the ![Select tool icon] **Select** tool.

5. (Optional)

    •   Rotate, zoom or pan your cropped photo. To help with the composition of your photo, see *Using the Rule of Thirds* on p. 86.

    •   Adjust the frame to fit the crop—see overleaf.

Adjusting frames

If a photo has been cropped inside a frame, you can adjust the size and shape of the frame to suit it. The frame can be, moved, rotated, resized and even recolored independent of the photo. You can even add an effect or color to the frame—without affecting the photo.

1. Select the framed photo with the ![cursor] **Select** tool.

2. Click ![frame icon] **Select Frame Object**.

3. To resize the frame, drag a handle. The frame's aspect ratio is preserved. To resize to any aspect ratio, hold down the **Shift** key while dragging.

4. (Optional) The **Select Frame Object** tool also lets you isolate the frame so you can add effects or change the frame's color—without affecting the photo inside it.

5. Click ↰ **Back** to return to the ➤ **Select** tool.

Rotating, zooming, and panning

1. Select the photo, and then click the **Crop** button.

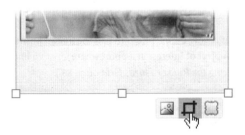

2. To rotate, or zoom into or out of the photo, click the buttons displayed at the right edge of the photo.

3. To pan the photo inside its frame, click and drag on the photo.

4. To use the **Rule of Thirds** to grid to help with your composition:

   • On the Crop context toolbar, click ⊞ **Show/Hide Thirds Grid**.

   • Click and drag on the photo to pan the image, positioning your main subject of interest at a point where any two lines intersect. (See *Using the Rule of Thirds Grid* on p. 86.)

5. To close the Crop window, click ⬑ **Back**, or click elsewhere on the page or pasteboard area.

Replacing a framed photo

- Drag a new photo from the **Photos** tab and drop it onto the frame. CraftArtist fits the photo to the frame automatically.

Changing a photo frame

- Drag a new frame from the **Frames** tab and drop it onto the photo. CraftArtist replaces the existing frame and fits the photo to the new frame automatically.

Deleting frames and framed photos

You can delete frames (along with the photos inside them) from your pages. You can also remove frames from the **Frames** tab.

Deleting frames from the page

- Select a frame and press the **Delete** key.

  If the frame contains a photo, this will also be deleted from the page.

Removing frames from the Frames tab

- On the **Frames** tab, select a frame and click its 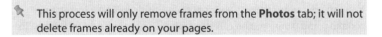 **Remove** button.

  This process will only remove frames from the **Photos** tab; it will not delete frames already on your pages.

Converting photos to frames

Photos you've added directly to your page (i.e., those that are not inside a decorative photo frame) can be converted so that they sit inside "frameless" frames.

Once converted, these frames function exactly like the decorative frames you've added from the **Frames** tab. For example, if you use the **AutoFlow** feature to automatically populate frames in your project, photos in frameless frames will also be replaced. (See *Using AutoFlow* on p. 109.)

> If you have used the Line tab to apply an outline or edge to your photo, when you convert the photo to a frame, the outline itself becomes the new frame. For information on applying outline and edge effects, see *Changing line style* on p. 174.

To convert a photo to a frame:

1. Select the photo with the **Select** tool.

2. On the context toolbar, click **Convert to Frame**.

   The photo is converted to a frame, and the ⬚ ⬜ ⬜ Frame controls display beneath it.

   Notice also that the Photo context toolbar has been replaced with the Crop context toolbar.

You can now adjust the way your photo fits inside its frame by rotating, zooming, and panning. You can also crop the photo and adjust its frame to follow suit. See *Fitting photos to frames* on p. 108.

Working
with text

You can create artistic text and shape text in CraftArtist. Both text types are fully editable, and you can apply formatting, styles, and color fills before or after typing.

> If you're looking to add decorative text to your project you should try adding Digikit **letters** from the **Digikit Browser** (see p. 53).

Text types overview

The following table outlines the main characteristics of artistic and shape text.

Text type	Use and characteristics
Artistic text 	• Great for decorative typographic design. • Individual letters can be stretched, rotated, sheared, and combined with other items.
Shape text 	• Lends itself well to blocks of body text where shape and flow contribute to the overall layout. • Conforms to the containing shape. You can't manipulate individual letters, but you can achieve unique text flow effects by varying the container's properties. • Shape text does not have a line property.

Adding artistic text

1. On the Standard toolbar, click the  **Text** tool.

2. To create text at the default size, click on your page to set a text insertion point.

   -or-

   Click and drag on your page to set the size of the text insertion point.

- To set text attributes before typing, adjust the settings on the Text context toolbar. (See *Formatting text* on p. 125.)

- To set text color before typing, set the **Line** and **Fill** swatches on the **Color** tab. (See *Changing line and fill color* on p. 219.)

3. Start typing. To start a new line of text, press the **Enter** key.

Adding shape text

1. Create a shape either from the QuickShape flyout or by closing a drawn line.

2. With the shape selected, start typing. Text flows within the shape and the **Text** tool is automatically selected.

To set text attributes before typing, adjust the settings on the Text context toolbar. (See *Formatting text* on p. 125.)

To set text color before typing, set the **Line** and **Fill** swatches on the **Color** tab. (See *Changing line and fill color* on p. 219.)

- (Optional) To start a new line of text, press the **Enter** key.

- If you've typed more text into a shape than it can display, an **Overflow** button displays below the shape when it's selected.

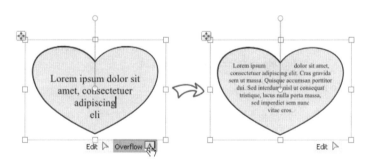

Click the **Overflow** button (or the **AutoFit** button on the Text context toolbar) to reduce the size of the text.

-or-

To reveal all the text without changing the font size, enlarge the shape.

- To extract text from a shape (as an artistic text item), right-click the shape and click **Detach as New Item>Text**. To detach the text from its containing shape, simply drag it.

Working with text on the page

To select an entire artistic or shape text item:

- Click it with the  **Select** tool.

To edit a text item:

1. Select the item with the **Select** tool, and then click the I-beam **Edit** button that displays below the item.

   -or-

   Select the item with the **A** **Text** tool.

   A text edit cursor is inserted inside the text.

2. Click and drag to select the text you want to edit, and then retype. See *Editing and deleting text* on p. 124.

To move a text item:

- Select it, and then drag it.

   -or-

   Click and drag its **Move** button.

To resize a text item:

- Select it and drag a corner resize handle.

To rotate a text item:

- Select it and drag its Rotate handle.

To apply text formatting:

- Select the text, and then adjust the settings on the Text context toolbar. See *Formatting text* on p. 125.

You can also rotate and shear text items, and apply shadows, transparency, and other effects. For details, see:

- *Rotating and shearing items* (p. 235)

- *Adding drop shadows* (p. 145)

- *Applying transparency* (p. 150)

- *Adding outlines to text* (p. 133)

- *Applying 2D filter effects* (p. 146)

You can also add frequently used text as a resusable **sentiment**. See Sentiments on p. 137.

Editing and deleting text

You can edit and delete artistic text and shape text directly on the page, or in the **Edit Text** dialog (for details on working in the **Edit Text** dialog, see CraftArtist Help).

To edit text on the page:

1. Select the item with the **Select** tool, and then click the **Edit** button that displays below the item.

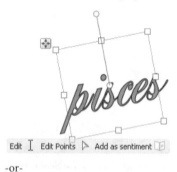

Edit Ⅰ Edit Points ▷ Add as sentiment ⬚

-or-

Select the item with the **A** **Text** tool.

2. A flashing text edit cursor is inserted inside the text.

3. Type new text at the insertion point, or click and drag to select the text you want to edit.

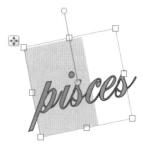

4. Type your new text.

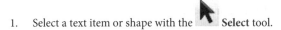

To cut, copy, and paste text, use the standard Windows keyboard shortcuts.

To delete an entire text item:

1. Select a text item or shape with the **Select** tool.

2. Press the **Delete** key.

To delete selected characters or words:

1. Select a text item or shape with the **Select** tool.

2. Click the **A** **Text** tool.

   A flashing text edit cursor is inserted inside the text.

3. Click and drag to select the text you want to delete, and then press the **Delete** key.

Formatting text

You can select and format artistic text and shape text directly on the page using the Text context toolbar, the **Format** menu, or the **Edit Text** dialog.

Selecting text for formatting

To format an entire text item:

1. Select the item with the 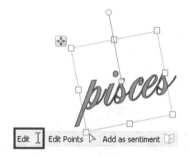 **Select** tool.

2. Use the Text context toolbar or **Format** menu to apply formatting, as described below.

To format selected letters or words:

1. Click the **A** **Text** tool, and then click and drag to select one or more characters or words.

2. Use the Text context toolbar or **Format** menu to apply formatting.

Using the Text context toolbar

The Text context toolbar lets you apply basic text attributes, such as point size, font style, alignment options, and so on, to selected text.

To format text from the Text context toolbar:

1. Select a text item, a character, or a group of characters.

2. On the Text context toolbar, adjust the settings described below:

- Select a font from the **Fonts** drop-down list.

> Lists font names and provides a preview of the selected text. Icons indicate the font type (e.g., **T** = TrueType).

- Select a text size from the **Point Size** drop-down list.

> Shows the height of the selected text in points.

- Click to apply bold, italic, or underline formatting.

- Click to apply left, center, right, or justified text alignment.

- Click to apply a bullet or numbered list style.

- Click to incrementally decrease or increase text indents.

- Click **AutoFit** to increase or decrease the size of shape text to fit its containing shape.

- Click to incrementally increase or decrease text size.

- Click to apply super- or subscript to text. A^x A_x

Superscript formatting is automatically applied to ordinates, e.g., the 'st' in 1st will change to 1st. See *Using Auto-Correct* in CraftArtist Help for more information.

- Click to display the **Curved Text** flyout. Click a preset path to apply it to a selected artistic text item.

You can only fit artistic text to a curve. See *Putting text on a path* on p. 130 for more information.

Using the Format menu

1. Select a text item, a letter, or a group of letters.

2. On the **Format** menu, click **Character**, **Paragraph**, **Tabs**, **Bullets & Numbering**, or **Text Flow**.

3. Make your changes in the respective dialog(s), and then click **OK**.

   See CraftArtist Help for a detailed description of these options.

For special adjustments on artistic text:

1. Select the text item with the **Select** tool.

2. Click the ▷ **Edit Points** button under the selected text.

   Adjustment sliders and handles appear to the left of, and above and below the text. Hover the cursor over a slider to see its function.

- Drag the WRAPPING (E) slider inward to change wrapping (how line wraps onto a new line).

- Drag the LEADING slider (A) to change leading (space between lines).

- Drag the LETTER SPACING slider (D) to change tracking (spacing between characters).

- To move a single character, select and drag the square handle at the character's lower-left corner (B).

💡 To constrain movement horizontally or vertically, select a letter and then press and hold down the **Shift** key while dragging the letter.

- To move a group of letters, select them one at a time with the **Shift** key held down.

- To rotate a single character (illustrated), click its handle and drag the node on the opposite end of the displayed line to either side (C).

Fitting text to a path

CraftArtist allows you to make artistic text conform to a curved baseline (such as a drawn freeform line or curve), custom shape or a preset shape (QuickShape).

Putting text on a path

To fit text to a path:

1. Select the curve or shape.

2. Click the **A** **Text** tool.

3. Hover over the curve or shape's outline until you see a ⌇∿ cursor, then click at the point on the line where your text is to begin.

4. Begin typing your text. The text will be placed along the curve or shape.

Alternatively:

1. Create your artistic text.

2. Create a freehand, straight, or curved line or a shape.

3. Select both objects and on the **Tools** menu, click **Fit to Curve**. The text now flows along the specified path.

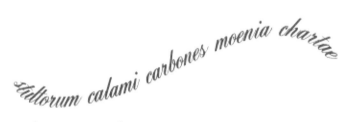

To flow text along a preset path:

1. Select your artistic text.

2. From the context toolbar, click the down arrow on the **Preset Text Paths** button and select a preset curve from the drop-down menu on which the text will flow.

Refining a text path

Artistic text on a path remains editable as text. Likewise, you can continue to edit its path using the **Edit Points** button as described in Editing lines and shapes.

When a path text object is selected, you'll notice that text paths have several unique "handles" not found on other objects. You may need to zoom in a bit, but it's easy to select the handles—special cursors let you know when you're directly over them. To see what the handles do, carefully compare these two examples:

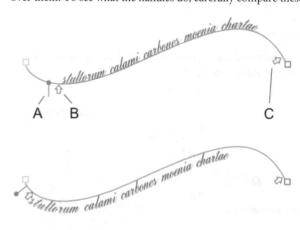

- The **Baseline Shift** handle (**A**), resembles a QuickShape handle with a tiny slider control.

  Drag the slider with the ⇕ cursor to raise and lower the text with respect to the path. In the bottom example, we've lowered the original text.

- The **Start** (**B**) and **End** (**C**) handles, look like arrows on the text path.

  Drag them with the ꜱᴛᴀʀᴛ and ᴇɴᴅ cursors to adjust where the text begins and ends with respect to the path's start and end nodes. In the bottom example, we've moved the start of the path to the left.

To edit a text path:

1. Select the text object.

2. Click the **A** **Text** tool to display the text path.

3. Drag the Baseline Shift handle to raise or lower the path and/or drag the Start and End handles to alter the start and end points.

Adding outlines and edges to text

You can create interesting text effects by adding various line, brush stroke, and "fringed" edge styles to your artistic text items.

> You cannot apply lines and edges to shape text.

Adding outlines to artistic text

1. Select a text item with the **Select** tool.

2. Open the **Line** tab.

3.   To apply a line style, click one of the following buttons:

Line tab button	Effect achieved
Solid	
Dash	
Double	
Calligraphic	

4. Adjust the line width by dragging the slider.

To remove an outline, click the ☐ **None** button.

Adding brush stroke edges to artistic text

1. Select a text item with the ▸ **Select** tool.

2. On the **Line** tab, click the 🖌 **Stroke** button.

3. On the **Brushes** tab, select a brush stroke style.

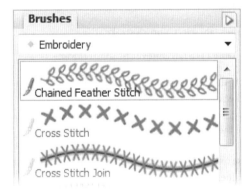

The stroke is applied to the text outline.

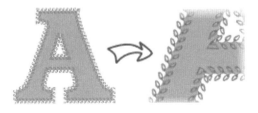

4. Use the following **Line** tab controls to adjust the effect:

    • Change the stroke width by dragging the slider.

    • Increase or decrease the flow of the brush stroke by changing the
       brush **Flow** value.

Adding fringed edges to artistic text

1. Select a text item with the ![Select tool] **Select** tool.

2. On the **Line** tab, click the ![Edge button] **Edge** button.

3. On the **Brushes** tab, select a brush stroke style.

4. Use the following **Line** tab controls to adjust the effect:

    • To apply the edge style *inside* the edge of the text, select the **Inner
       Edge** check box.

    • Change the stroke width by dragging the slider.

    • Increase or decrease the flow of the brush stroke by changing the
       Flow value.

Adjusting the outline distance

Use the **Line** tab's **Offset** value to change the distance between a text item and its
outline.

To adjust line offset:

1. Select a text item with the  **Select** tool.

2. On the **Line** tab, adjust the **Offset** value to achieve the desired effect.

   You can click the up/down arrow buttons; click the right arrow button and drag the slider; or type a value and press **Enter**.

Sentiments

If you're always stuck for words, CraftArtist can help you add sentiments and quotes to your designs with just a few simple clicks!

You can create a new sentiment from any artistic text object. In fact, you can even create a single sentiment from several text objects! This makes it really easy to design and use complex text designs over and over again quickly and easily!

Adding sentiments to the page

1. On the page context toolbar, click  **Insert Sentiment**.

   -or-

   On the **Insert** menu, click **Sentiment or Quote...**

2. In the **Insert sentiment or quote** dialog:

   - In the left pane, select the category and/or sub-category that fits your design.

   - In the right pane, click on the sentiment that you want to use.

   - Click **Insert**.

3. To create the sentiment at the default size, click on your page.
   -or-

   Click and drag on your page to set the size of the sentiment.

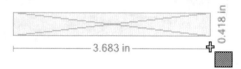

4. The sentiment is added as an artistic text object(s).

Editing sentiments on the page

Once you have added your sentiment to the page, it behaves in the same way as any other artistic text object. See the help topics contained within **Working with Text** in the Table of Contents for further details.

Creating new sentiments

1. Create and select your artistic text object(s).

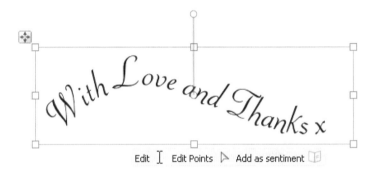

Edit ⊺ Edit Points ▷ Add as sentiment 📖

> Why not start with an existing sentiment and then personalize it as we've done in this example?

2. Click the 📖 **Add as sentiment** button.

3. In the **Create new sentiment or quote** dialog, select the category (indicated by a yellow folder icon) into which you want to add the sentiment, then:

    •   Select and existing sub-category and click **Add > Add to existing**.
        -or-

- Type a name for the new sub-category and click **Add** > **Add New**.

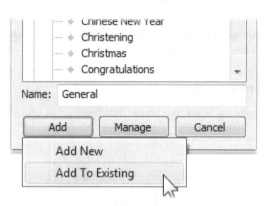

To create an entirely new category for your sentiments, see **Managing sentiments** in CraftArtist Help.

4. Your new sentiment will now be available from the **Insert sentiment or quote** dialog.

Having a party or two? You can also use sentiments to quickly create advance text layouts. In our example, we used several text objects to create this standard invitation sentiment.

Please come to my party!

On:

....

at

....

....

....

RSVP

....

Applying effects

Adding drop shadows

The **Shadow Tool** is great for allowing freeform control of a drop shadow effect. With its on-the-page control nodes and supporting Shadow context toolbar, the tool offers various adjustments such as Opacity, Blur, and X (or Y) Shear.

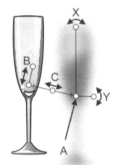

Simple shadow	**Offset**	**Skewed**
(drag from item center)	**shadow**	**offset shadow**
	(adjusted origin)	(adjusted Origin and X
	A - Origin of shadow	Shear)
	B - Blur	
	C - Opacity	
	X - X-axis shear	
	Y - Y-axis shear	

💡 Once you've created a basic shadow, you can further edit it as needed using the Filter Effects dialog.

Applying drop shadows with Shadow Tool

1. Select the item and click the ▢ **Shadow Tool** on the **Standard** toolbar. Control nodes display to allow for shadow adjustment, as illustrated above.

2. Drag across the item to create a drop shadow.

3. Change blur, opacity, or shear properties by dragging the respective control nodes (or via the displayed context toolbar).

To change a shadow's color:

- Select the item, choose the **Shadow Tool**, then select a color from the **Color** tab.

To remove the shadow from an item:

- Double-click the item while the **Shadow Tool** is selected.

Applying other 2D filter effects

Changing material depth

If you've manipulated materials you've added to the page, perhaps by cutting out with the **Scissors** tool, you can apply some depth by applying an embossing effect.

- On the Effects tab, adjust the **Material Depth** setting. (The greater the value, the more pronounced the embossed effect.)

Material Depth

24 pt ▸

Making feathered edges

Feathering applies a softer edge to design items such as embellishments or cut materials. The effect also looks great when applied to photo edges.

- In the lower-right corner of the Effects tab, enter a **Feather Edge** value.

  (This is the distance inside the item's outline from which feathering will be applied.)

Feather Edge

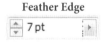

 The Feather option in the **Filter Effects** dialog (see CraftArtist Help), offers independent control of **Opacity** and **Blur**, which can also be used in conjunction with other 2D filter effects.

Applying 3D filter effects

As well as 2D filter effects, CraftArtist provides a variety of **3D filter effects** that you can use to transform any item. Such effects are selectable from an Effects tab which offers an impressive choice of ready-to-go simulated natural and manufactured surfaces. When applied to drawn items, previously "flat" appearances are brought to life by application of depth and texture.

The **Effects** tab displays a variety of thumbnail presets in various categories (Glass, Metal, Animals, etc.).

Click any thumbnail to apply it to the selected item.

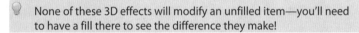

None of these 3D effects will modify an unfilled item—you'll need to have a fill there to see the difference they make!

Paper textures

Paper textures simulate various real media textures of varying roughness and "feel", such as **Canvas, Cartridge, Embossed, Parchment,** and **Watercolor.**

As a paper texture is a layer property, the layer's texture is applied to all items on that layer. A different texture can only be applied to a different layer (and to all its items).

Applying paper textures

1. On the Layers tab, select the layer on which to apply a paper texture.

2. Click the **Paper Texture** button displayed after the chosen layer's name.

3. In the **Bitmap Selector** dialog, select the **Paper Textures** category. A gallery of texture thumbnails displays.

4. Choose a thumbnail and adjust **Scale** and **Opacity** values if required.

5. Click **OK**.

On the **Layers** tab, the layer's **Paper Texture** button changes to , indicating that a paper texture has been applied.

All existing items on the layer, and any new items added to the layer, will adopt the applied paper texture.

Removing a paper texture

1. On the **Layers** tab, locate the layer whose texture you want to remove and click the **Paper Texture** button.

2. In the **Bitmap Selector** dialog, click the **Remove** button. The paper texture is removed from the layer and all items on it.

You can also switch, edit, and remove paper textures from within the **Layer Properties** dialog. (Right-click on a layer entry, choose **Layer Properties**, and then click **Edit**).

Applying transparency

Transparency effects are great for highlights, shading and shadows, and for simulating realism. They can make the critical difference between flat-looking illustrations and images with depth and snap.

Transparency may seem a bit tricky because you can't "see" it the way you can see a color fill applied to an item. In fact, it's there all the time in CraftArtist. Each new item has a transparency property: the default just happens to be "None"—that is, no transparency (opaque).

Transparencies work rather like fills that use "disappearing ink" instead of color. The more transparency in a particular spot, the more "disappearing" takes place there, and the more the item(s) underneath will show through.

For example, in the illustration below, the butterflies have a solid (100% opaque) transparency, a gradient (100% to 0% opaque) transparency and a solid (50% opaque) transparency from left to right.

Solid transparency distributes the transparency equally across the item. **Gradient** transparencies are created by drawing a path across the item; Linear transparencies are drawn by default but other categories such as **Radial**, **Ellipse**, **Conical, Plasma, Square, Three Points**, and **Four Points** can be created.

Applying solid transparency

The **Color** tab hosts a **Transparency** slider that controls the level of **solid** transparency applied to currently selected items.

The further right the slider, the more opacity; the further left the more transparency. Remember that opacity is the inverse of transparency—100% Opacity = 0% Transparency and vice versa.

To apply solid transparency from the Color tab:

1. With your item(s) selected, go to the **Color** tab.

2. Adjust the **Transparency** slider to set the level of transparency. The transparency is applied to the selected item(s) uniformly.

Applying gradient transparency

Just as a gradient fill can vary from light to dark, transparency can be applied as a opacity gradient, by drawing a gradient transparency path across the item. The gradient transparency path links the **From** and **To** nodes (e.g., from 100% opacity (black node) to 0% opacity (white node)).

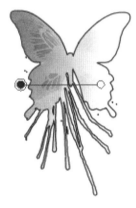

For items with a gradient transparency applied, you can adjust the transparency effect by adding or subtracting nodes along the gradient transparency path.

The **Transparency Tool** displays an item's gradient transparency, indicated by two or more nodes situated along a path. You can reposition the nodes to adjust the transparency's starting point or end point.

For transparencies with multiple nodes, you can also adjust the intermediate levels of transparency. Each node has its own value, comparable to a key color in a gradient fill (see *Applying gradient fills* on p. 222). Each selected node's value can be altered directly on the page or in the Gradient Transparency Editor dialog.

To apply gradient transparency with Transparency Tool:

1. Select an item.

2. Click the ![icon] **Transparency Tool** on the **Standard** toolbar.

3. To apply a simple Linear transparency (grading from 100% opacity to 0% opacity), click and drag across the item to define the transparency path.

    The effect starts where you place the start node, and ends where you place the end node.

Changing transparency type

By default, the **Transparency Tool** applies a simple linear transparency on the drawn path. However, the tool's context toolbar lets you change to one of several transparency, e.g., Radial, Conical, Ellipse, Plasma, etc.

The path's appearance may change to reflect the transparency type, but the principles of editing the transparency path are the same.

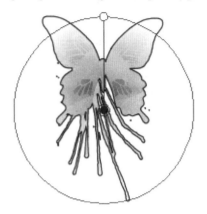
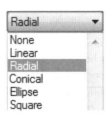

Editing gradient transparency

Once you've applied a gradient transparency, you can adjust its **path** on the item, and the **level** of transparency along the path. You can even create more complex transparency effects by adding extra nodes to the path and assigning different values to each node.

Each node along the path is selectable by clicking and can therefore adopt its own transparency value.

To adjust the transparency path:

1. Select the item with a gradient transparency applied.

2. Click the **Transparency Tool** on the **Standard** toolbar.

3. Drag the displayed nodes to new positions. You'll notice the effect change as you drag a node.

Editing a **gradient transparency** path is similar to editing a solid gradient fill path (see *Editing gradient fills* on p. 224). Adding a level of transparency means varying the transparency gradient by introducing a new **node**, and assigning the node a particular value. For transparencies with multiple nodes, each node has its own value, comparable to a key color in a gradient fill.

You can either edit the path directly using the **Transparency Tool**, or use the Gradient Transparency Editor dialog (similar to the Gradient Fill Editor). Both methods let you define key values along the path.

The **Gradient Transparency Editor** dialog lets you fine-tune the actual spread of transparency between pairs of key values, and displays the transparency gradient, with pointers marking the nodes (corresponding to nodes on the path) that define specific transparency values. Again, black represents 100% opacity, and white represents 0% opacity, with grayscale values in between. A sample window at the lower right shows the overall transparency effect.

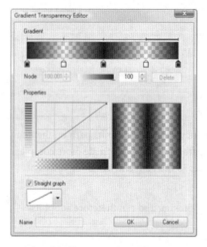

For details of how to edit and manage transparency in the **Gradient Transparency Editor** dialog, see CraftArtist Help.

To edit gradient transparency directly:

1. Select the item, then the  **Transparency Tool** button from the Standard toolbar. The item's transparency path appears, with start and end nodes.

2. To add a transparency node, hover over the path until the cursor changes then click on the point on the path where you want to add the node.

3. To change the grayscale/transparency value of any existing node, including the start and end nodes, select the node and move the Color tab's transparency slider to the required value.

4. To move a node you've added, simply drag it to a new position along the transparency path.

5. To delete a node you've added, select it and press **Delete**.

Adding lines
and shapes

Using QuickShapes

The QuickShapes flyout provides a wide variety of commonly used shapes that you can instantly add to your page.

To create a QuickShape:

1. Click ![Shapes icon] **Shapes** on the **Standard** toolbar and select a shape from the flyout.

2. On your page, either:

   - Double-click to place a default-sized QuickShape.

     -or-

   - Click and drag to draw your QuickShape at a specific size. To constrain the aspect ratio (for example, to obtain a square or circle), hold down the **Shift** key while dragging.

> New QuickShapes adopt the currently set line and fill, as defined on the Color tab. See *Changing fill and line color* on p. 219.

Once you've drawn your QuickShape, you can adjust its properties—for example, apply solid fills (p. 220), gradient fills (p. 222), or transparency effects (p. 221). You can even use sliding **control handles** to create variations on the original QuickShape.

You can also use the QuickShape context toolbar, situated above the workspace, to swap QuickShapes and adjust line weight, color, style, and more.

All QuickShapes can be positioned, resized, and rotated. What's more, you can adjust their appearance as soon as they are drawn, or at a later time.

To adjust the appearance of a QuickShape:

1. Select the item with the ![Select tool icon] **Select** tool.

2. Click the ![Edit button icon] **Edit** button displayed beneath the item. This reveals sliding round handles around the shape. (Different QuickShapes have different handles.)

3. Drag the handle to change the appearance of a QuickShape.

For example, dragging the top sliding handle to the right on the Quick Star below will produce a very different star shape.

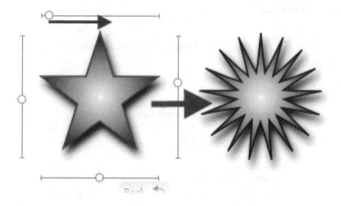

Drawing lines and shapes

You can draw straight or curved lines. As soon as you draw a line you'll see its **points** appear. The line between any two points is called a **line segment**. Freeform and curved lines usually have many points; straight lines have only two.

All lines and line segments have **line properties** such as **color** and **weight** (thickness). For details on applying color to lines and shapes, see *Changing line and fill color* on p. 219.

When a line, or series of line segments, forms a complete, enclosed outline, it becomes a new **closed** item called a **shape**. Because shapes can be filled with a solid or gradient fill, they have **fill properties** as well as line properties.

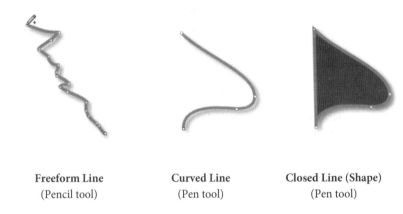

Freeform Line	**Curved Line**	**Closed Line (Shape)**
(Pencil tool)	(Pen tool)	(Pen tool)

Drawing freeform lines

1. Click the  **Pencil** tool on the **Standard** toolbar.

2. Click once, then drag across the page, drawing a line as you go. The line appears immediately and follows your mouse movements.

3. To end the line, release the mouse button. The line will automatically smooth out using a minimal number of points. Note the dots indicating its points—at the two ends, and at each point where two line segments come together.

4. (Optional) To set the degree of smoothing to be applied to the line (and subsequent lines), set the **Smoothness** value (by entering a value or adjusting the slider) on the context toolbar.

To draw a straight line, hold down the **Shift** key down as you drag.

Drawing curved lines

Curved lines are created as a series of connected line segments (which may be curved or straight) using a series of "connect the dots" mouse clicks. New line segments are added all the time. The tool is designed for drawing complex, combination curves and shapes in a highly controlled way.

1. Choose the ✒ **Pen** tool from the **Standard** toolbar.

2. From the displayed context toolbar, choose to create your drawn

    segments in ⌢ **Smooth joins** or ⌃ **Sharp joins** creation mode. By
    default, you'll be in **Smooth joins** mode.

3. Click where you want the line to start (**1**).

4. Click again for a new point and drag out a pair of **control handles**
    which orbit the point (**2**). (Control handles act like "magnets," pulling
    the curve into shape. The distance between handles determines the
    depth of the resulting curved line.) Release the mouse button to create
    your curve segment (**3**).

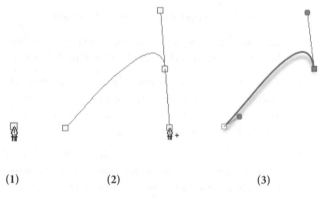

| (**1**) | (**2**) | (**3**) |

5. To extend an existing line, click beyond the end of your current curve
    to create a new point (thus creating another curve segment). Normally,
    curve segments end in a symmetric (evenly rounded) corner (**4**), with
    control handles locked together.

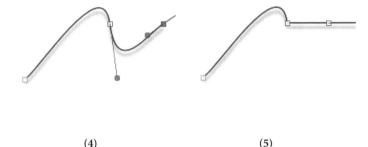

| (4) | (5) |

6. However, you can press the **Alt** key while drawing the segment to define a "cusp" or sharp corner (**5**). This locks the control handle on the last created point. For more on line corners, see *Editing lines and shapes* on p. 164.

7. To end the line, press **Esc** or choose a different tool.

Drawing shapes

To close a freeform line or curve as you draw:

•   For irregular shape, simply extend the line back to its starting point. Shapes have an interior which is filled with the current **default fill** (see *Changing line and fill colors* on p. 219) when the line or curve is closed.

To close an existing line or curve (with a straight line):

1. Select the line or curve with the ![Select tool] **Select** tool (**Standard** toolbar).

2. Click the ![Edit Points] **Edit Points** button displayed beneath the item.

3. Select ![Close Curve] **Close Curve** button from the context toolbar. A Straight segment appears, closing the curve.

If you're trying to draw a cartoon outline made up of many independent curves (e.g., a cartoon ear, rose, etc.) you may want to fill each curve without closing it. This is made easy by using the **Fill-on-Create** feature.

To fill an unclosed curve automatically:

1. Select the **Pencil**, **Pen**, or **Brush** tool (**Standard** toolbar).

2. On the context toolbar, click to enable  **Fill-on-Create**, and then select a fill from the **Color** tab.

3. Draw a freeform line and the resulting curve will automatically fill with the current fill color.

Editing lines and shapes

All items, lines, and shapes are composed of one or more **line segments** (which can be straight or curved) that are joined at their **points**. To edit a line or shape, you can manipulate its segments and/or points, redraw lines, reshape lines (by moving or adding/deleting points), or join two or more lines together.

To:	Do this:
Move a whole line	Using any selection tool, drag the line.
Redraw part of a line	Draw a new portion with the **Pencil** tool while in **Editing** mode.

Extend a line	Drag away from a node, creating a new segment.
Reshape a line (or curve)	Drag points while in **Editing** mode.
Simplify a line (remove points)	Adjust the **Smoothness** setting on the **Pencil** tool's context toolbar.
	Select and delete points while in **Editing** mode.
	Use Clean Curves to remove unwanted points.
Enhance a line (add points)	Click anywhere on a line segment while in **Editing** mode.
Change the type of point or line segment	While in **Editing** mode, select a point then pick a different segment from the context toolbar.
Convert to straight line segments	Click the **Straighten Line** or **Convert to Straight Lines** buttons (Context toolbar).
Adjust a shape	Drag points while in **Editing** mode, and/or adjust control handles.
	Use the context toolbar to break open the shape, then add line segments.
Join two lines together	Select two lines, then choose **Join Curves** from the **Tools** menu.

Redrawing part of a line

You can use the **Pencil** tool to redraw any portion of a line or curve.

To redraw part of a selected line:

1. Select the line, then the  **Pencil** tool. Hover the displayed cursor over the line, at the point where you want to begin redrawing.

    The cursor changes to indicate you can begin drawing.

2. Click on the line.

3. Keep the mouse button down and drag to draw a new line section, connecting it back to another point on the original line. Again, the cursor changes to include a curve when you're close enough to the line to make a connection.

    When you release the mouse button, the original portion is replaced by the newly drawn portion.

Extending lines

Any kind of open line (that is, one that hasn't been closed to create a shape) can be resized. You can use any of the line tools to do so.

To extend a line:

1.   Select the drawn line with the ![Select tool] **Select** tool, and then select the line's drawing tool.

Move the cursor over either of the end points, a small + cursor will appear. Click at that location.

Drag out to draw a freeform line beyond the end point.

The line that you create will be a continuation of the existing line, as a new line segment.

You can optionally close the curve, creating a new shape that can take a fill!

Reshaping lines

To reshape a line, you can drag or adjust its points and segments.

> To reshape a straight line segment, first convert it to curves (see *Converting a shape to editable curves* in CraftArtist Help).

To reshape a curved line:

1. Select the line with the **Select** tool.

2. Click the ▷ **Edit Points** button displayed beneath the item. The line's points appear, and a context toolbar displays. (Some of the toolbar's buttons may be 'grayed out.' These will become available when you select a point or part of the line/shape to work on.)

3. Either:

   • Hover over a segment and drag the segment to form a new curve shape.

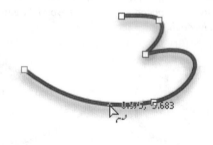

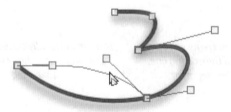

-or-

- Hover over a point (the cursor will display) and click to select the point. Optionally, **Shift**-click or drag out a marquee to select multiple points.

Control handles (in blue) for the adjacent line segment(s) will appear.

Note that each segment in the line has a control handle at either end, so when you select an **end point** or **interior point**, you'll see either a control handle on each selected end point (one segment) or a pair of handles at a selected interior point (two segments), respectively.

Drag any selected point to reshape adjacent segment(s). All selected points move in the same direction, so you can reshape the curve by selecting specific points. (**Shift**-drag to constrain the movement to horizontal or vertical.)

Drag one or more control handles to change the curvature of the line on either side of a point. You can shorten or lengthen the handles, which changes the depth of the **curve**, or alter the handle angle, which changes the curve's **slope**.

> By changing the type of point you can change how the adjacent segments behave.
>
> As a shortcut when selecting points, you can press **Tab** or **Shift-Tab** to select the next or previous point along the line (following the order in which points were created).

Simplifying or enhancing lines and shapes

The more points there are on a line or shape, the more control over its shape you have. The fewer points there are, the simpler (smoother) the line or shape. You can adjust smoothness to refine the curve most recently drawn (as long as the line is still selected).

To adjust the smoothness of the most recent pencil line:

1. Click the ✏️ **Pencil** tool and draw a freeform line.

2. On the context toolbar, click the right arrow on the **Smoothness** option and drag the displayed slider left or right to increase or decrease the number of points (you can also type absolute values into the input box).

    The line is made less complex, i.e., smoother, by dragging the slider to the right to decrease the number of points.

To add a point to a line or curve:

*   If the line is selected with the drawing tool used to create it, single-click (for a pen line) or double-click (for a pencil line) on the line to add a new point.

    -or-

*   If the line is not selected, select it with the ▲ **Select** tool, click ▷ **Edit Points**, and then single-click on the line to add a new point.

    The new point is created and selected by default.

To delete a point:

1. Select the line with the ![icon] **Select** tool, and click ![icon] **Edit Points**.

    -or-

    Select the line with the ![icon] **Pen** tool.

2. On the context toolbar, click ![icon] **Delete Point** (or press the **Delete** key).

You can also reposition the points, and reshape the line or shape, by dragging on its control handles (see below).

If you've converted a shape to curves you can clean up unwanted points by using the **Clean Curves** command. See *Converting a shape to editable curves* in CraftArtist Help.

Changing points and line segments

Each segment in a line has a control handle at either end, so at each interior or "corner" point (where two segments join) you'll see a pair of handles.

The behaviour of these handles—and thus the curvature of the segments on either side—depends on whether the point is set to be **sharp**, **smooth**, **symmetric**, or **smart**. You can quickly identify a point's type by selecting it and then checking to see which button is selected on the displayed context toolbar.

Each type's control handles behave differently as illustrated in the table below.

To change one or more points to a different type:

1. Select the item with the ![icon] **Select** tool.

2. Click the ![icon] **Edit Points** button displayed beneath the item, then click on the point you want to change (**Shift**-click or drag out a marquee to select multiple points).

3. Click one of the point buttons on the displayed context toolbar:

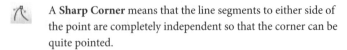

A **Sharp Corner** means that the line segments to either side of the point are completely independent so that the corner can be quite pointed.

A **Smooth Corner** means that the slope of the line is the same on both sides of the point, but the depth of the two joined segments can be different.

At a **Symmetric Corner**, points join line segments with the same slope and depth on both sides of the point.

> Normally, custom segments you draw with the Pen tool end in a symmetric corner.

Smart Corner points automatically determine slope and depth for a rounded, best-fitting curve.

If you attempt to adjust a smart corner's handles, it changes to a smooth corner. You can always reset the point to smart—but to maintain smart points, be careful what you click on!

You can also use the context toolbar to define a line segment as either straight or curved.

To change a line segment from straight to curved, or vice versa:

1. While in Editing mode, select the leading point of the line segment (the point nearer the start of the line).

2. Then, either:

    *   To make a line segment straight, click **Straighten Line** on the context toolbar. The selected segment immediately jumps to a straight line.
        -or-

    *   To make a line segment curved, click one of the point buttons (describe above) on the context toolbar: **Sharp Corner**, **Smooth Corner**, **Symmetric Corner**, or **Smart Corner**. You can then adjust the curvature of the newly created curved segment.

To convert to straight lines:

1. While in Editing mode, select the curve.

2. On the context toolbar, choose ⌃ **Convert to Straight Lines**. The curve segments are replaced by straight line segments throughout the line.

Adjusting a shape

As described previously, you can easily turn a curve into a shape by connecting its end points. You can go the other way, too—break open a shape in order to add one or more line segments.

To break open a line or shape:

1. Select the item with the ▲ **Select** tool.

2. Click the ▷ **Edit Points** button displayed beneath the item.

3. Select the point on the closed curve where you want the break to occur.

4. Click the ┣┱ **Break Curve** button on the context toolbar so that the line will separate. A shape will become a line, with the selected point split into two points, one at each end of the new line.

5. You can now reposition the points and reshape the line by dragging on the handles.

> 🖎 When you first break a curve the two points are in exactly the same location and so the curve may still look as if it is connected. If you drag one of the red point ends away you will quickly see the separation.

> 🖎 If the broken shape had a fill you can change the unwanted fill to be transparent by using the Color tab's Fill swatch.

Joining lines

You can connect any two straight or curved lines to form a new line.

To join two lines together:

1. Select both lines by **Shift**-clicking with the  **Select** tool.

2. Choose **Join Curves** from the **Tools** menu. The end control point of one line is connected with the start control point of the other.

Changing line style

All lines, including those that enclose shapes, have numerous properties, including color, style, line ends, weight, join, cap, and offset.

Using the Line tab, you can adjust **plain line** properties for any freeform, straight, or curved line, as well as for the outline of a shape or photo.

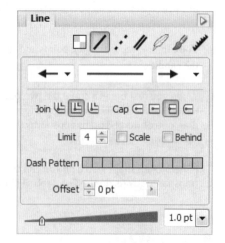

Changing line color

Color swatches present in a Digikit automatically become available in the **Color** tab when it is loaded. For details on adding or editing plain line colors, see *Changing fill and line color* on p. 219.

Changing line style

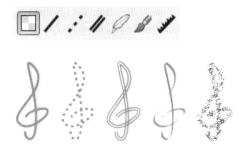

A series of buttons arranged along the top of the **Line** tab set the line style.

Solid, **Dash**, **Double**, **Calligraphic**, and **Stroke** styles can be applied.

A fringed **Edge** style can also be applied to shapes, text, and photo edges.

To change line style:

- Click a button to set the line style—only one style can be set at any one time. Click another button to jump to that style.

Once a style is selected you can choose line ends for most styles (except **Stroke** and **Edge**).

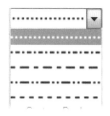

For some styles, variations are also available.

For example, for a **Dash** or **Double** line style, additional dash patterns (below) and double line options can be selected.

To select a line end:

- From the  and drop-down menus, pick a line start and end.

Other styles such as **Dash** and **Calligraphic** offer further customization of the chosen style.

Two styles, **Stroke** and **Edge**, let you apply a brush, chosen from the Brushes tab, to the edge of a shape or edge. You'll see your current brush shown on the **Line** tab. Both styles look great when applied to artistic text. (See *Adding outlines and edges to text* on p. 133.)

For changing line caps and ends, see CraftArtist Help.

Changing line width

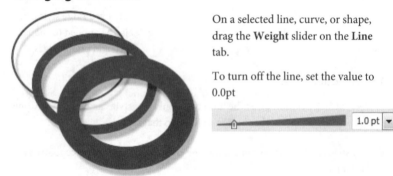

On a selected line, curve, or shape, drag the **Weight** slider on the **Line** tab.

To turn off the line, set the value to 0.0pt

Adjusting line offset

On a selected line, curve, or shape, adjust the **Line** tab's **Offset** value. This lets you adjust the distance between an object, brush stroke, etc., and its outline. To do this, you can click the up/down arrow buttons, type a value directly, or click the right arrow and drag the slider.

Copying an item's formatting

Use **Format Painter** to copy an item's line and fill properties directly to another item (you can even copy between line/shape and text items).

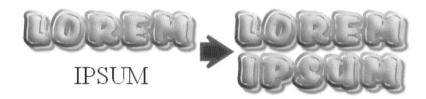

 The Format Painter is particularly useful if you've taken the time to fine-tune an item's appearance (e.g., you may have applied a complex fill or combination of filter effects), and want to apply the same format to other items on your page.

To apply an item's formatting to another:

1.   Select the item whose formatting you wish to copy.

2.   Click  **Format Painter** on the **Standard** toolbar. When you click the button, the selected item's formatting is "picked up."

3.   Click the item to which you want to apply the "picked up" formatting. The second item becomes selected and the formatting is applied.

- To cancel Format Painter mode, press **Esc**, click on a blank area of the page, or click any other tool button.

- While in Format Painter mode, to select an item *without* pasting formatting, hold down the **Shift** key and then select the item.

- When copying formatting from one text item to another, text properties such as font and style are also passed along.

Scissor cuts, crops, and erasing

Scissor cuts

Use the **Scissors** tool to cut any item or group of items on your page. For example, you might want to cut a material or embellishment, or add a decorative cut edge to a photograph.

You can cut freeform shapes, or apply a preset "punch" shape.

Cutting freeform shapes

1. Use the 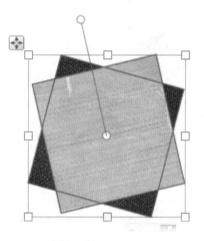 **Select** tool to select one or more items.

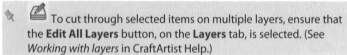

To cut through selected items on multiple layers, ensure that the **Edit All Layers** button, on the **Layers** tab, is selected. (See *Working with layers* in CraftArtist Help.)

2. On the **Standard** toolbar, click the **Scissors** tool.

3. On the Scissors context toolbar, select a scissor type from the drop-down list.

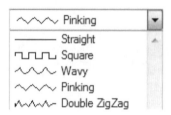

4. Optional:

    • To adjust the regularity of the freeform cutting line, adjust
       the **Smoothness** setting.

To do this, click the up and down arrows, or click the right arrow and
drag the slider.

• To adjust the length of
   each unit of the cutting
   edge, change the
   Wavelength setting.

• To adjust the depth of
   each unit of the cutting
   edge, change the
   Amplitude setting.

You can't adjust
wavelength or
amplitude for **Straight**
cutting lines.

5. To create a freeform cut, click and drag across the item(s).

✎ Unselected items that the cutting line crosses will **not** be split.

6. To remove a cut section, click it.

-or-

To retain a cut section, hold down the **Shift** key, and then click the section you want to retain. (All other portions of the item will be deleted.)

-or-

To retain both sections and split them apart:

- Click the ![] **Select** tool and then click a cut section.

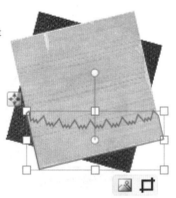

- Drag the section into its new position.

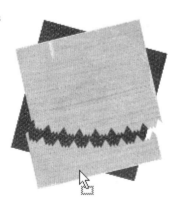

Punching shapes

1. Use the 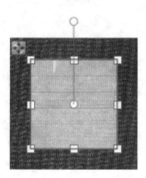 **Select** tool to select one or more items.

2. On the Standard toolbar, click the 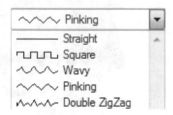 **Scissors** tool.

3. On the Scissors context toolbar, select a scissor type from the drop-down list.

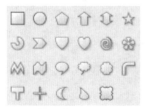

4. Click to expand the **Punches** flyout, and then click a preset punch shape to apply it to your item.

5.   The punch is applied to the item. Click the **Cut** button that displays below the item.

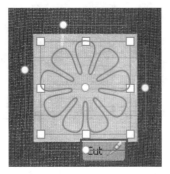

6.   To delete or retain cut sections:

  •   To delete a cut section, click it.

  •   To retain a cut section, hold down the **Shift** key, and then click the section.

- To retain both sections and split them apart, click the  **Select** tool, then click a cut section and drag it into its new position.

Combining, cropping, and joining items

CraftArtist provides the powerful **Combine**, **Crop**, and **Join** (**Add**, **Subtract**, and **Intersect**) commands, which you can use on multiple selections to create new shapes.

For easy access to these commands, use the buttons on the **Arrange** tab. You'll also find these commands on the **Arrange** menu, and from the menu accessed by right-clicking on a multiple selection.

Combining items

Combining merges selected items into a composite item, with a hole where filled regions overlap. The composite takes the line and fill of the bottom item.

1. Use the 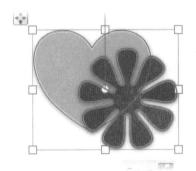 **Select** tool to create a multiple selection containing the items to be combined.

2. On the **Arrange** tab, click the **Combine** button (you'll also find this option on the **Arrange** and right-click menus).
   The composite takes the line and fill of the back item.

> ✄   To break apart the item, select it and click the button again.
>
> ✄   You can also use the **Crop** tool to crop photos and other items on your page. See *Cropping photos* on p. 85.

Cropping items

1.   Use the ▲ **Select** tool to create a multiple selection containing the items to be cropped.

2.   On the **Arrange** tab, click the ⊕ ▼ **Crop** button to display a flyout.

3.   To crop the bottom item to the outline of the top item, select **Crop to Top**.

-or-

To crop the top item to the outline of the bottom item, click **Crop to Bottom**.

> ✄   To remove the crop, click **Arrange>Crop>Uncrop**.

Clipping items

1. Use the **Select** tool to create a multiple selection containing the items to be clipped.

2. On the **Arrange** tab, click the down arrow to expand the **Crop** flyout.

3. To clip the bottom item to the outline of the top item, click **Clip to Top**.

-or-

To clip the top item to the outline of the bottom item, click **Clip to Bottom**.

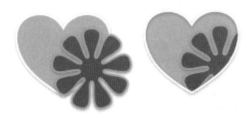

To remove the clip, click **Arrange>Crop>Uncrop**.

Adding items

Adding creates a new item that's the sum of two or more selected items, whether or not they overlap.

1. Use the  **Select** tool to create a multiple selection of items. (The items need not overlap.)

2. On the **Arrange** tab, click **Add**.

   The new item is a composite of the selected items, taking the line and fill of the bottom item.

Subtracting items

Subtracting creates a new item, retaining only the portion of the bottom item that is not overlapped. This command is particularly useful for cutting out shapes from photos.

1. Use the  **Select** tool to create a multiple selection of overlapping items. (The items must overlap.)

2. On the **Arrange** tab, click Subtract.

The new item consists of the non-overlapping portion(s) of the bottom selected item.

Intersecting items

Intersecting creates a new item by retaining the overlap and discarding the rest.

1. Use the ![Select tool] **Select** tool to select two overlapping items.

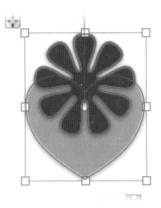

2. On the **Arrange** tab, click ![Intersect icon] **Intersect**.

The new item consists of the overlapping portions of the previously selected items, taking the line and fill of the back item.

✎ **Add**, **Subtract**, and **Intersect** produce a permanent new item out of any selected items. You can only break the resulting item apart *immediately* after creating it by clicking the **Undo** button on the **Standard** toolbar.

Erasing and adding to items

Erasing   Adding to

CraftArtist provides the following tools for erasing and adding to existing lines and shapes.

 Erase Tool

Lets you erase portions of a selected item or items. You can control the extent of erasing by setting eraser tip width and pressure (if using a graphics tablet).

 You can erase on an individual layer or across multiple layers. (See *Working with layers* in CraftArtist Help.)

 Freeform Paint Tool

Lets you add to or 'grow' the boundary of an existing shape or line. This tool is especially useful for reshaping existing items, or for creating unusual filled shapes.

 If you add to or erase from a bitmap, QuickShape, or artistic text item, the item will be converted to curves, preventing further editing in their original form.

Erasing portions of an item

1. Use the **Select** tool to select an item.

2. On the **Standard** toolbar, click the ⬜ **Erase Tool**.

3. On the context toolbar, choose an eraser tip shape.

4. (Optional) Set the tip width by adjusting the **Width** value.

5. Position the cursor, and drag over the item's edge. The area to be erased is drawn temporarily (use the **Ctrl** key to redefine the erase area while drawing).

6. Release the mouse button to erase the area drawn.

The erasing process shows the background color belonging to any item behind it (either on the same layer or a layer below the current layer).

Adding to an item

1. Use the **Select** tool to select an item.

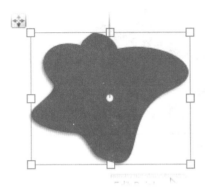

2. On the **Standard** toolbar, click the 🖌 **Freeform Paint Tool**.

3. On the context toolbar, choose a shape for the tool's tip.

4. (Optional):

   • Set the tip width by adjusting the **Width** value.

   • To create a series of shapes without switching tools, click to disable the 🔲 **Select-on-Create** button.

5.   Position the ⬭ cursor over the item and drag over an item boundary.

You'll see dark shading, which represents the area to be added.

6.   Release the mouse button to reshape the item to include the painted area.

Using stencils

The **Stencils** tab provides a selection of ready-to-go, fun stencils that will add impact to any page. Whether you paint over them with the **Brush** tool, or use them to cut out a design from a photo, stencils provide endless opportunities for creativity.

Adding stencils to your page

1. On the **Stencils** tab, select a category from the drop-down list.

   The lower gallery displays thumbnails of the stencils available in the selected category.

2. Click and drag a thumbnail from the gallery onto your page.

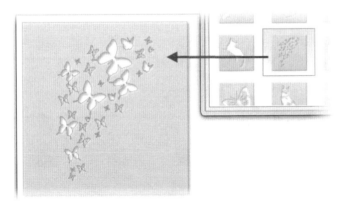

Painting over stencils

1. Add a stencil to you page.

2. Click the  **Brush** tool.

3. Choose a brush type from the **Brushes** tab and set your brush color on the Color tab. (See *Adding brush strokes* on p. 207.)

> 💡 Brushes in the Airbrushes, Glitter and Natural Media categories are particularly suited to stencil work.

4. Paint over the stencil with your chosen brush.

> 📌 By default, stencils are set up so that paint is applied to the inner edge. To switch to the outer edge, click **Outer**.

5. Click  **Lift Stencil** to remove the stencil and reveal the painted design beneath it.

Cutting out a stencil from a photo

1. Add a stencil to you page.

2. Drag a photo from the **Photos** tab and drop it on top of your stencil.

3. Position the photo so that it displays as required inside the stencil outline.

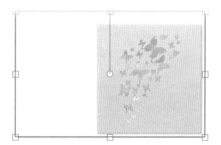

4. Select the stencil and click ✎ **Lift Stencil** to remove the stencil and reveal the cut out design beneath it.

Adding brush strokes

Adding brush strokes

Add artistic flair to your projects with the ![brush icon] **Brush** tool.

The Brushes tab provides a wide range of brushes. Choose from preset, categorized **Global** brushes, or add **Digikit** brushes to your workspace.

You can draw and paint with your mouse or with a pen tablet. The tablet's pressure-sensitive pen tip allows control of stroke width or transparency (see *Pressure sensitivity* in CraftArtist Help).

Choosing brush types

Brush types

The **Global** category provides the following  natural stroke and  spray brushes:

- **Airbrushes**
  Add dramatic, soft, or textured airbrush effects.

- **Edges**
  Apply inner or outer edge effects to any shape or picture.

- **Embroidery**
  'Stitch' items to your page with these colorful brushes.

- **Flowers**
  Paint your pages with flower spray brushes.

- **Fun & Celebrations**
  Create cheerful, fun layouts with confetti, sweets, and clouds.

- **Glitter**
  Make your pages sparkle with glitter dust and glitter glue brushes.

- **Grunge**
  Add aged and grunge effects to your layouts.

- **Natural Media**
  Apply paint (dry, medium, and watery), acrylic, charcoal, pastel, pen, and watercolor natural media brush strokes.

- **Photo**
  Add realistic lace, rope, ribbon, and rope effects with this collection of photo brushes.

- **Special Effects**
  Paint with bubbles, fire, snowflakes, splats, and more!

Selecting brushes from the Brushes tab

The Brushes tab lets you view brushes currently being used in your project, and serves as a container for supplied brush presets, brushes from Digikits, and your own custom brush designs.

Document category

The **Document** category shows the brush types used in the currently active project.

This category is useful for automatically 'bookmarking' brushes for easy reuse.

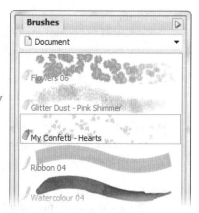

Global category

The **Global** category stores the supplied brush presets under a series of pre-defined subcategories.

These brushes are available to all projects currently open.

Digikit category

The **Digikit** category displays brushes added from free or purchased Digikits you've chosen in the **Digikit Browser**. Most Digikits contain brushes, but some may not by design.

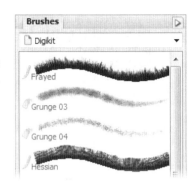

Adding brushes from Digikits

1. On the Pages context toolbar, click **Add items from Digikits**. The **Digikit Browser** dialog opens.

2. In the **Digikit Browser**, select the Digikit from which you want to add brushes.

3. Scroll to the **Brushes** category (if present), and then hover over the brush you want to use to. If you like the brush, double-click the preview to add it. To add all brushes from the Digikit, click **Add all items** at the top right of the category pane.

   When a brush is added, a check mark appears on the brush thumbnail.

⊿ Picnic in the Park

> If you select a brush from a featured free or purchasable Digikit—
> the **Digikit Not Installed** dialog will display and you will be
> prompted to visit the DaisyTrail.com shop. Once you've installed
> your free or purchased Digikit, the brush will be added to the
> **Digikit** category of the **Brushes** tab on selection. (See *Buying
> Digikits* on p. 57.)

4. (Optional) Click  **Back to 'All Digikits'** to add brushes from other Digikits.

5. When you've finished selecting brushes, click **Done**.

Creating brush strokes

You can apply brush strokes directly to the page using your mouse or pen tablet.
If you're using a pen tablet, you can control stroke width and transparency by
adjusting pressure sensitivity (see *Pressure sensitivity* in CraftArtist Help).

Applying brush strokes

1. On the **Standard** toolbar, click the ![brush] **Brush** tool.

    The Brush cursor (![cursor]) indicates that the Brush is selected and that you're ready to paint.

2. On the **Brushes** tab, choose a brush category from the drop-down list, and then select a brush stroke style from the gallery.

    At the top of the workspace, notice that the Brush context toolbar is displayed. Use the controls on this toolbar to set the properties of your brush stroke, as described in steps 3 to 6 below.

> The following steps provide an overview of the brush properties. For more details, see *Setting brush stroke properties* on p. 214.

3. Click the ![icon] **Color** button and select a brush stroke color using the **Color Selector** dialog.

4. Set the **Width**, **Opacity**, and **Smoothness** of your brush stroke. Click the up and down arrows, or click the right arrow and then drag the slider.

5. (Optional) Enable the ![icon] **Fill-on-Create** button if you want to fill your closed or unclosed shape as you paint. (See Setting brush stroke properties.)

6. (Optional) Enable the ![icon] **Select-on-Create** button if you want to be able to edit your strokes immediately after painting them.

7. With the brush cursor drag a brush stroke across your page.

> The properties currently defined on the Brush context toolbar settings will be adopted for subsequent brush strokes.

A brush stroke can be extended or reshaped, as for a straight or curved line (see *Editing lines and shapes* in CraftArtist Help). The brush stroke path can also be reversed, closed, or opened.

Setting brush stroke properties

You can set the properties of your brush strokes (both before and after creating them) using the Brush context toolbar.

To set brush stroke properties:

1. To set properties before painting, click the ![brush] **Brush** tool and choose a brush style from the Brushes tab.

    -or-

    To set properties of an existing brush stroke, select the stroke.

    The Brush context toolbar displays.

    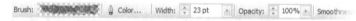

2. To change the brush design, select a category on the **Brushes** tab.

3. To change the brush color:

    -   Set the line swatch on the Color tab. (See *Changing line and fill colors* on p. 219.)

        -or-

    -   Click the ![color] **Color...** button on the context toolbar, and then choose your color from the **Color Selector** dialog. See *Using the Color Selector dialog* in CraftArtist Help.

> ✎ Brush strokes cannot take a gradient fill. If applied, the base color of the fill is adopted.

4. To change brush stroke width:

    •   Adjust the **Width** setting on the context toolbar (you can enter a value; click the up/down arrows; or click the right arrow and then drag the slider).

        -or-

    •   At the bottom of the Line tab, drag the slider or enter a value in the adjacent box.

5. To adjust brush stroke opacity:

    •   Adjust the **Opacity** setting on the context toolbar. (100% opacity = no transparency; 0% opacity = fully transparent.)

        -or-

    •   On the Color tab, drag the **Transparency** slider to achieve the desired effect.

6. If, in step 1, you selected the **Brush** tool rather than an existing brush stroke, you'll see three additional options on the context toolbar: **Smoothness**, **Select-on-Create**, and **Fill-on-Create**.

    •   **Smoothness:** Adjust the degree of smoothing to be applied to the brush stroke by entering a value; clicking the up/down arrows; or clicking the right arrow and then dragging the slider.

    •   **Select-on-Create:** Click to enable or disable this option.

Select-on-Create disabled:
When you release the mouse button, the stroke you just created is not selected. This means that if you want to edit or add to the stroke, you must first select it. Use this method when you're happy to set all your brush stroke properties *before* painting—and particularly if you intend to paint repeatedly with the same brush stroke style.

Select-on-Create enabled:
When you release the mouse button, the curve or stroke you just created is automatically selected, allowing you to add to or edit it immediately. Use this method when you want to change your brush stroke properties (color, width, opacity, etc.) frequently.

 Press the **Esc** key to deselect the current brush stroke.

- **Fill-on-Create:** Enable if you want to fill the unclosed curve produced with a brush stroke with the fill color defined on the **Color** tab. (See *Changing line and fill colors* on p. 219.)

Working
with color

Changing fill and line color

You can apply colors to the outline and interior of closed shapes and text objects, and to lines and line segments.

In the **Digikit Browser**, the **Swatches** category (shown when browsing items) offers a selection of colors specifically chosen to complement your installed Digikits. Once a Digikit is selected, these colors become available in the **Digikit** palette, which displays on the Color tab.

To apply fill and line color, you can:

- Select a swatch from the Digikit palette. (See below.)

- Apply a color tint or a transparent fill. (See below.)

- Use the Color tab's **Color Picker** to apply a color used elsewhere on your page. (See below.)

- Use the Color tab's Color Wheel, Color box, or sliders. (For more on the Color tab, see CraftArtist Help.)

- Mix a custom color in the **Color Selector** dialog. (See *Using the Color Selector dialog* in CraftArtist Help.)

- Apply a gradient fill. (See *Applying gradient fills* on p. 222.)

- Apply a plasma or mesh fill. (See CraftArtist Help.)

Applying colors from the Digikit palette

1. Select a shape, line, or text object.

2. On the **Color** tab:

    *   To change line color, click to select the **Line** swatch.

    *   To change fill color, click to select the **Fill** swatch.

3. Click a palette swatch previously loaded from a Digikit (via Digikit Browser). The color is applied and the **Line/Fill** swatch updates with the selected color.

    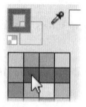

    For information on switching palettes, see *Using color palettes* on p. 226.

Applying color tints

1. Select a shape, line, or text object.

2. On the **Color** tab:

    *   Click to select the **Line** or **Fill** swatch, as described in step 2 above.

    *   In the Color Mode drop-down list, select **Tinting**.

3. Drag the  slider to the right to lighten the tint, or to the left to darken the tint.

   You can also enter a percentage value in the box (0% resets to the original color).

Applying transparent fills

1. Select a shape, line, or text object.

2. On the **Color** tab, click to select the **Line** or **Fill** swatch, as described above.

3. On the **Color** tab, click the ▣ **No Fill** swatch.

> This applies transparency to items with line/fill properties, such as shapes and text. For pictures, clicking this swatch resets a recolored picture back its original colors. See also *Applying transparency* on p. 150.

Applying colors with the Color Picker

1. Select a shape, line, or text object.

2. On the **Color** tab:

   - Click to select the **Line** or **Fill** swatch, as described above.

   - Click the 🖉 **Color Picker**.

3. On your page, click on your chosen pickup color with the pickup cursor (to magnify the color swatch, hold down the mouse button).

4. The color is picked up and displayed in the 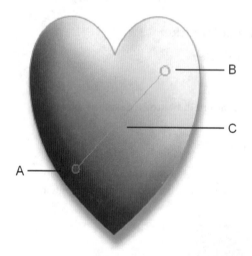 **Picked Color** swatch.

5. On the **Color** tab, click the **Picked Color** swatch to apply the color.

6. **Optional:** To add the color to your **Document** palette, click the **Color Tab Menu** button and select **Add to Palette**. (See also *Using color palettes* on page 226.)

Applying gradient fills

Gradient fills include the **Linear, Radial, Ellipse, Conical, Square, Three Color, and Four Color** types. All of these apply color 'spectrums' in a **fill path** spreading between two or more **nodes**. Once you've applied a gradient fill, you can edit its fill path and change its colors.

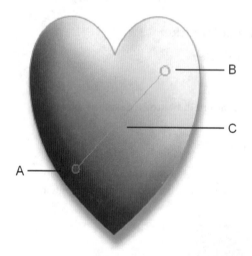

*(**A**) Start Node, (**B**) End Node, (**C**) Fill Path - Linear*

Applying a gradient fill

1. Select an item on your page.

2. Click the **Fill Tool**.

3. Click and drag on the item to define the fill path. The item takes a simple **Linear** fill, grading from the current color of the item, ending in white (items filled with white will grade from white to black, to show contrast).

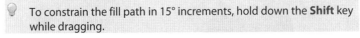

To constrain the fill path in 15° increments, hold down the **Shift** key while dragging.

4. Optional: To change the fill style, choose from the drop-down list on the Fill context toolbar.

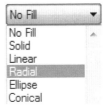

The new fill path displays. Note that this will differ depending on the fill style selected.

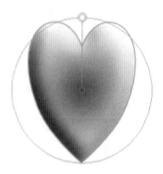

Editing a gradient fill path

1. Select an item with a gradient fill applied.

2. Click the ![Fill Tool icon] **Fill Tool** to display the fill path.

3. Move the fill path nodes by clicking and dragging them.

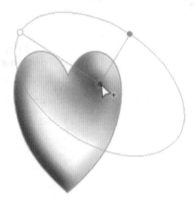

-or-

Click and drag across the item to define a new fill path.

To constrain the fill path in 15° increments, hold down the Shift key while dragging.

To ensure that the origin of the gradient remains at the item's center point, hold down the **Ctrl** key while dragging.

Adding and deleting fill path nodes

1. Select an item with a gradient fill applied.

2. Click the 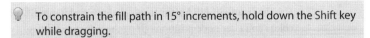 **Fill Tool** to display the fill path.

3. To add a node, click anywhere on the fill path.

    -or-

    To delete a node, click to select it and then press the **Delete** key.

Changing node colors

1. Select an item with a gradient fill applied.

2. Click the 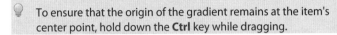 **Fill Tool** to display the fill path.

3. Use any of the following methods to recolor fill path nodes:

    •   For a simple gradient fill with two nodes, choose from the **Fill Start** and **Fill End** palettes on the context toolbar.

    •   For fills with three or more nodes, select a node on the fill path, and then choose from the **Fill Color** palette on the context toolbar.

    •   Select a node and then on the Color tab, click a color swatch. See *Editing gradient fills* in CraftArtist Help.

    •   Right-click the filled item and choose **Format>Fill...** (or choose the command from the **Format** menu).

Use the **Gradient Fill Editor** to add/remove nodes, modify node colors and alter node positions along the path. See *Editing gradient fills* in CraftArtist Help.

> Adjustment techniques, Fill Tool, and context toolbar options differ depending on the fill style.

Using color palettes

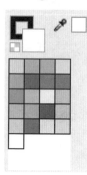

When you apply a **solid fill** or **line color**, you choose a color belonging to a color **palette**.

Only one palette can be active at any one time. The currently active palette is displayed as a gallery of swatches on the Color tab.

You can add, edit, and remove palette colors, and switch between different palettes at any time. You can also create your own custom palettes from color spreads. (See *Creating custom palettes* in CraftArtist Help.)

> Changes to palettes are saved globally and the new palette colors are automatically carried over to any new projects you create.

The following palette types are available:

- **Digikit palette:** These palette colors originate from your chosen Digikit—you'll see the **Color** tab populate with Digikit colors when you select a Digikit for your new Craft Project (see p. 21 and p. 220).

  You can modify your **Digikit palette** at any time via the **Digikit Browser**—select the **Browse my items** tab, then the **Swatches** category to add or remove colors to the current Digikit palette by clicking! (See below.)
  Note: Some Digikits may not contain palette colors, in which case the default **Document** palette is displayed on the **Color** tab.

- **Document palette:** If you start a blank project from scratch, rather than from a Digikit, the default **Document** palette is displayed on the **Color** tab. This palette provides a set of commonly-used colors from which to choose.

  You can edit the colors displayed in the **Document** palette—for example, you may want to add swatches from a Digikit or a themed palette, or add a color you have mixed yourself on the Color tab or Color Selector dialog. You can also save your **Document** palette for use in other projects.

- **Standard RGB** and **Standard CMYK palettes:** Palettes based on industry-standard color models.

- **Themed palettes:** CraftArtist also provides a range of designer-created themed palettes containing colors designed to work well together on the page.

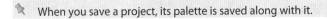 When you save a project, its palette is saved along with it.

Switching palettes

1. On the **Color** tab, click **More...**

2. In the **Color Palette Designer**, the Palettes drop-down list displays all of the palettes installed with CraftArtist.

3. Click the palette you want to use.

   The selected palette's colors appear as swatches in the **Color Palette Designer** and on the **Color** tab, replacing the swatches previously visible.

Adding swatches to the Digikit palette

1. On the context toolbar, click  **Add items from Digikits**.

2. In Digikit Browser, click the **Browse my items** tab.

3. In the category list on the left, click **Swatches**.

4. Swatches already added to your **Digikit** palette are highlighted in the main window.

5. You can remove colors from the palette, and add colors from other installed Digikits.

    ●   To remove a color from the palette, click to deselect it.

    ●   To add a color, click to select it.

6. Click **Done**. Colors are automatically removed from/added to the **Digikit** palette displayed on the **Color** tab.

7. **Optional:**

    ●   To add the color to your **Document** palette, click the ▷ **Color Tab Menu** button and choose **Add to Palette**.

        (You would do this if you intended to save your **Document** palette for use in other projects, for example.)

See also *Editing palette*s on p. 230.

Changing Document palette colors

You can add colors manually from the Color tab, or take them directly from an item's fill. Once a color is stored in the **Document** palette, you can edit it in the Color Picker dialog.

To add a color from an item's fill to the Document palette:

- Select an item that has a fill color you want to add to your palette, then click the ▷ **Color Tab Menu** button and select **Add to palette**.

To add a color manually from the Color tab:

1. On the Color tab:

   - Click the **Fill** swatch, and then click to select your preferred color.

   -or-

   - Click the ⚲ **Color Picker**, hold down the mouse button, and then click anywhere in your workspace to pick up your new color.

     Click the ⚲☐ **Picked Color** swatch to transfer the color to the **Fill** swatch.

2. Click the ▷ **Color Tab Menu** button and select **Add to palette**.

Editing palettes

To add a new palette swatch:

1. On the **Color** tab, right-click on the palette and click **Add**.

2. In the Color Selector dialog, choose your new color and click **OK**. (See *Using the Color Selector dialog* in CraftArtist Help.)

   The color is added to the currently loaded palette.

3. **Optional:** To add the color to your **Document** palette, click the ⮞
    Color Tab Menu button and choose **Add to Palette**.

    (You would do this if you wanted to save your **Document** palette for
    use in other projects, for example.)

To edit a palette swatch:

1. On the **Color** tab, right-click on the swatch you want to edit and click
    Edit.

2. Follow step 2 above.

To remove a palette swatch:

•   On the **Color** tab, right-click on the swatch you want to remove and
    click **Delete**.

Saving palettes

To save the currently active palette (the palette displayed on the Color tab):

1. On the **Color** tab, right-click the palette and select **Palette Manager**.

2. In the **Palette Manager** dialog, click the **Options** button, and select
    Save Palette As.

3. Save the palette to a new *.plt file.

To save a different palette:

1. On the **Color** tab, click **More...**

2. In the **Color Palette Designer**, in the Palettes drop-down list, select
    the palette you want to save.

3. Click **Save**.

4. Save the palette to a new *.plt file.

> 🖱 By default, palette files are saved to the **Palettes** folder of your
> installation directory.

If you store your palette to a different location, it will not appear in the **Palettes** drop-down list. To use a palette that is not saved in the **Palettes** folder, you need to load it.

Loading other palettes

In the **Color Palette Designer**, the drop-down **Palettes** list lets you quickly switch to any of the palettes saved in the **Palettes** folder. However, you can also load palettes that are stored elsewhere on your computer.

To load a palette:

1.   On the **Color** tab, click **More...**

2.   In the **Color Palette Designer**, click **Load**.

3.   Navigate to and select the palette you want to load.

4.   Click **Open**.

The loaded palette's colors appear as swatches in the **Color Palette Designer** and on the **Color** tab, replacing the swatches previously visible.

Arranging items

Aligning and distributing items

You can arrange, align, and distribute the items on your page quickly and easily. The resulting alignment of items differs depending on how you select the items.

Selecting items for alignment

Shift-click

- If you select items by holding down the **Shift** key and then clicking each item in turn, the items are aligned relative to the edges of the last selected item.

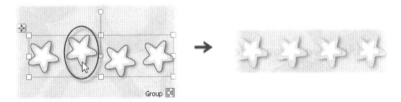

Selection marquee

- If you click and drag a selection marquee around the items to be aligned (or click **Edit>Select All**), the items are aligned relative to the item that is farthest back in the Z-order (the order in which items are placed on top of each other on the page).

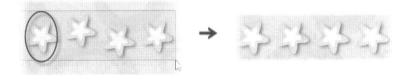

Alignment controls

Alignment controls are available on the **Align tab** or from the **Arrange>Align Items** menu item.

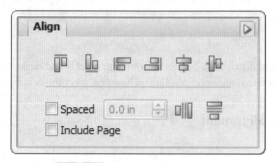

 Distribution controls let you distribute items evenly (you can set the space between items if required).

You can also distribute items across your page by selecting **Include Page**. See *Distributing items* on p. 237.

Aligning two or more items

1. On the **Standard** toolbar, click the ▶️ **Select** tool.

2. Press and hold down the **Shift** key, and then click to select all the items you want to align.

-or-

Click and drag a selection marquee around the items.

-or-

Click **Edit>Select All** to select all items on the page.

3. On the **Align** tab, select an option for vertical or horizontal alignment.

Aligning items with a page edge

Follow the steps above, selecting the **Include Page** option. The page is
added to the set of items included in the alignment, e.g., selecting
Align Top aligns all of the items in the selection to the top of the page.

 If only one item is selected, page-edge alignment is automatic.

Distributing items

1. On the **Standard** toolbar, click the ![Select tool] **Select** tool.

2. Press and hold down the **Shift** key, and then click to select all the items
   you want to align.

   -or-

   Click and drag a selection marquee around the items.

   -or-

   Click **Edit>Select All** to select all items on the page.

3. On the **Align** tab, click ![Horizontal Distribute] **Horizontal Distribute** or ![Vertical Distribute] **Vertical
   Distribute** to distribute items horizontally or vertically.

4. (Optional) To set a fixed distance between vertically or horizontally
   distributed items, select the **Spaced** option and enter a measurement
   value (otherwise the items distribute evenly between end-most items).

Rotating and shearing items

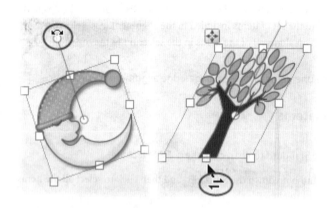

Rotating items

1. Select the item(s) with the **Select** tool.

2. Hover over the rotate handle, when you see the cursor change, drag in the direction in which you want to rotate the item.

    As you drag, the angle of rotation is temporarily displayed around the item's origin point (shown as ○). This temporary display of information is known as **tool feedback**.

    20.00°

    ⚲ To rotate in 15° intervals, press and hold down the **Shift** key while dragging.

    ⚲ To revert the rotation, double-click the rotate handle.

To change the rotation origin point:

1. Click and drag the origin point to any position on the page. (This can be outside the item itself—useful for rotating grouped items around a central point.)

2. Drag the repositioned rotate handle. The item rotates about the new origin point.

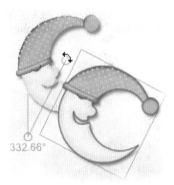

Additional rotation options are provided on the **Arrange** and **Transform** tabs, and on the **Arrange** menu. For details, see CraftArtist Help.

Shearing items

1. Select the item(s) with the  **Select** tool.

2. Hover over a center edge handle. When you see the Shear cursor, click and drag in the direction in which you want to shear the item, and then release.

- To copy and shear an item, press and hold down the **Ctrl** key while dragging—this preserves the original item, while shearing the new copied item as you drag.

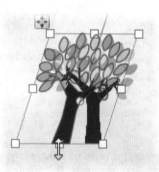

- For precise shearing, enter an exact **Shear** value in the Transform tab.

Ordering items

The items on your page are 'stacked' on top of each other, the front-most item (e.g., lilac flower above) being the one on top of the stack (also known as **Z-order**).

Each time you create a new item, it is placed in front of the items already there. You can move any item to any position in the ordering sequence using the buttons on the **Arrange tab** below. The lilac flower in the second illustration above has been moved to the back.

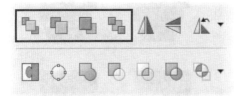

Equivalent commands are available from the **Arrange** menu's **Order** items submenu.

To change an item's position:

On the **Arrange** tab, click one of the following buttons:

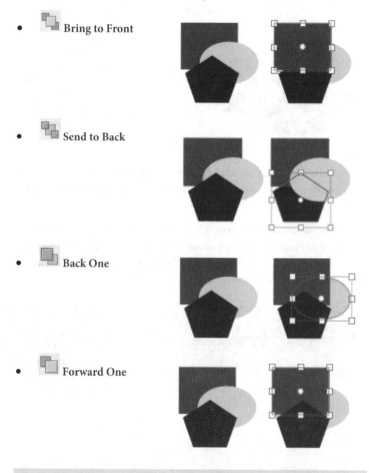

- **Bring to Front**

- **Send to Back**

- **Back One**

- **Forward One**

✎ Alternatively, ordering is possible using the right-click **Order Items>** options.

✎ Don't confuse the concept of item ordering with that of page layers. (See *Working with layers* in CraftArtist Help.)

Grouping items

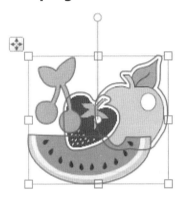

Grouping items prevents you from accidentally altering them.

Grouping also allows you to move, rotate, and resize items all together, and to edit similar items all at the same time.

You can select multiple items at the same time but this is a temporary operation; grouped objects are always kept together until you physically ungroup them. The only requirement for grouping is that multiple items are selected in advance. (See *Selecting, moving, and resizing items* in CraftArtist Help.)

To create a group from a multiple selection:

- Click the **Group** button below the selection.

To ungroup (turn a group back into a multiple selection):

- Click the **Ungroup** button below the selection.

In general, any operation you carry out on a group affects each member of the group. For example, property changes applied to a group—such as changing line or fill—will affect all the items contained in the group.

Sharing and publishing

Sharing via website

You can share your project by print, via email, as a distributable electronic PDF, or via the **daisytrail.com** website.

Publishing to DaisyTrail lets you contribute to the growing collection of published projects, and share your work with friends, family, and like-minded crafters!

To share your projects via website, simply complete the following steps:

- Register on the website.

- Login with your DaisyTrail account information in CraftArtist.

- Upload your chosen project.

The **www.daisytrail.com** website is designed specifically as a digital crafting community.

Main website features include:

- **Free stuff**
  Daisytrail.com offers free Digikits for you to download which are often seasonal, based on events, or on occasions.

- **DaisyTrail shop**
  Buy and download **individual Digikits** or entire **Digikit Collections**, plus font collections, software, and other goodies.

- **Commend and comment!**
  Praise and comment on other people's projects—and have your own designs assessed by the community. Click the **like this** button to commend your favorite projects.

- **Search**
  Find projects, groups, or other users throughout the website.

- **Make new friends!**
  Social networking meets craft designing! Use **email** or user discussion **forums** to build friendships with other crafters, especially those you add to your friends list.

- **Work in groups**
  Create groups of users with similar interests—great for schools, clubs, or maybe just your network of "crafty" friends.

Registering

1. Click  **DaisyTrail Upload** on the **Standard** toolbar.

2. If you've not registered before, click the **Join Now!** button. You'll be taken directly to **www.daisytrail.com** registration.

3. From the registration form, enter your personal information, including an email address to which an activation message will be sent. If you need **Help**, use the link provided.

4. Click **Create Account**. For account activation, you'll need to check your email and click on the activation message sent to you. This may take time depending on your ISP and connection.

 Remember your Username and Password. You'll need to re-enter this information into CraftArtist.

5. Registration is complete after activation. All you need to do now is to create your craft project and upload it!

If you don't add your DaisyTrail user account details, you'll be reminded to do so every eight days. You can register on the website, then transfer your username and password over, or cancel to enter your details later.

Uploading

Once you've successfully created your account you can upload your project, with the option of including only specific or all pages.

☑ Page 1

☑ Page 2

☑ Page 3

To upload your project from CraftArtist:

1. Click **DaisyTrail Upload** on the **Standard** toolbar.

2. If you've registered (see above) and are uploading for the first time, enter the **Username** and **Password** you created on DaisyTrail. You won't need to do this again on subsequent uploads.

3. In the dialog, uncheck pages you don't want to upload (use the scroll bar to view all pages).

4. (Optional) For the upload you can choose a different account to upload to. Click **My Account** and enter a different **Username** and **Password**.

5. Click **Upload** to transfer your selected pages.

6. On upload, a progress bar indicates upload status.

   On completion, click **OK** to close the dialog or click **View** to immediately see your uploaded project on the website.

Modifying account details in CraftArtist

1. Select **Options...** on the **Tools** menu.

2. In the **Upload** pane, enter your remembered **Username** and **Password**.

3. (Optional) Click the **Test** button to verify that the account details are correct. If successful, a "*Username and password valid*" message is displayed.

   If you've forgotten your password or you've not already registered, use the accompanying **Reset Password** and **Register** buttons. For the latter, you'll be directed to the **Registration** page on the website. Complete the registration details and click **Create Account**.

4. (Optional) Reduce the upload **Quality** to 96 DPI to speed up file transfer if your Internet connection is 56k dial-up modem (at the expense of zoom quality).

   Otherwise, use the default 300 DPI for broadband and all other faster Internet connections.

Basic printing

CraftArtist supports printing directly to a physical printer (e.g., All-in-ones, Inkjet and Laser printers), with options for scaling and thumbnail printing.

Greeting cards (below), scrapbooks, and other projects can be printed quickly and easily.

To print:

1. Click **File>Print...** (or right-click on the page or pasteboard area and click **Print**).

2. In the **Print** dialog, select a target printer from the drop-down list. Click the **Properties** button to set up the printer for the correct page size, etc. Set the page size from the **Advanced** tab if needed.

3. (Optional) If you want to create a print-ready *.prn file for printing at a later date, select the **Print to file** option.

4. Select the print range to be printed:

    • **Document**: Exports the whole project.

    • **Current Page**: Exports only the page currently displayed.

- **Pages**: Enter a page range (e.g., 3-5) to export a limited selection of pages (or individual page numbers, if separated by commas). If you've set a range, you can further export just odd or even pages in the range from the drop-down list.

- **Selection**: If you've selected an item in advance, you can print it in isolation using this option.

5. Enter the **Number of Copies** to be printed.

6. Check **Crop Marks** to add marks to the corner of your design when printing onto paper larger than your project's paper size. The marks indicate where to cut your design out after printing (using scissors, guillotine, etc.).

7. Choose a **Print Size** option:

- **As in document** (default). Prints the project without scaling to fit the paper. If your project uses a paper size larger than that currently set for the printer, the resulting printed output will 'cut off' parts of your page.

- **Shrink to fit paper size**. Reduces the print size to fit the printer's currently set paper size.

- **Scale to fit paper size**. Reduces or enlarges the print size automatically to fit neatly on the printed page, taking printer margins into account.

- **Best Fit**. CraftArtist scales the print size to prevent any unwanted white borders around your design from being printed. This makes full use of your printable area.

- **Print as thumbnails**. Prints multiple pages at a reduced size on each printed page, taking printer margins into account. Specify the number of thumbnails per sheet in the **Per sheet** value box.

8. Click **Print**.

The Preview window lets you review your print output before actually printing. It shows how your project pages map to the selected paper size. You can also choose **Print Preview** from the **File** menu.

Printing folded craft projects

If you've chosen a Greeting Card or Stationery craft project then the template you've chosen will automatically be set up to print your pages in the correct order, i.e. automatic **imposition** occurs.

Using purchased print media

For greeting cards, you'll probably want to use your own purchased card stock to print onto. For successful printing, you can either choose a print scaling option (p. 252) or you can use Page Setup (click **File>Page Setup**) to ensure the project matches the card stock used (by changing project layout and/or page size).

Using standard printer paper

If you're not using card stock, it's possible to make your own greeting cards from standard printer paper.

As an example, printing an A5 greeting card project to a desktop A4 printer, would output project pages 2 and 3 on the first printed sheet, with pages 1 and 4 on the second.

To create a double-sided card, it's popular to use the printer's manual feed to print the first printed sheet then flip this sheet over. Hey presto, you've got an double-sided A5 greeting card.

If you're happy to scale your project's paper size to your printer's default paper size (e.g., A4), you can choose **Scale to fit paper size** on the Print dialog when you print.

 You may prefer to use the manual feed in any case if you're using thicker than usual print media such as card.

Exporting as PDF

The cross-platform **Adobe PDF** file format is a worldwide standard for document distribution, which works equally well for electronic or paper publishing. It excels as an electronic distribution medium as it is device- and platform-independent.

To make sharing easy, you can export your project as a PDF file (Acrobat 4.0 compatible). In doing so, all the colors you've used will be output to an RGB color space, and all your pages will be rasterized (converted to bitmaps) on export.

Exporting as a PDF file

1. Click **File>Export>Export as PDF...**

2. In the dialog, select a **Print Range**:

   - **Entire document**: Exports the whole project.

   - **Current page**: Exports only the page currently displayed.

   - **Pages**: Enter a page range (e.g., 3-5) to export a limited selection of pages (or individual page numbers, if separated by commas). If you've set a range, you can further export just odd or even pages in the range from the drop-down list.
   For facing page spreads, enter the page number combination, e.g., 2, 3.

3. (Optional) Set other options as follows:

   - For more convenient on-screen viewing in Adobe Reader, specify how your project will initially appear by selecting the **Fit to complete page** or **Fit to page width** check box.

   - By default, your PDF file will display in your currently installed Adobe Reader immediately after export finishes. If you do not want to preview your file immediately after export, clear the **Preview PDF file** check box.

4. Select a **Print Quality** level from the drop-down list.

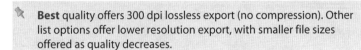

Best quality offers 300 dpi lossless export (no compression). Other list options offer lower resolution export, with smaller file sizes offered as quality decreases.

5. Click **OK**.

6. Choose a location and file name for your PDF file. Click **Save**.

   Once export completes, the PDF displays if **Preview PDF file** was selected in step 3 above.

Sharing via email

You can share your projects via email, attached as a JPEG or PDF*, or as your original *.craft project.

To share your project via email:

1. On the **File** menu, click **Send...**

2. In the **Send** dialog, choose the format in which to send your project.

   You can attach your project as a *.craft project file, as a JPEG image, or as a PDF document.

3. Your project is attached to a new email message, which opens in your default email program.

4. Just add your email recipient(s) and message and send your project!

Index